DEMOCRATIC METHODISM
IN AMERICA

DEMOCRATIC METHODISM IN AMERICA

A TOPICAL SURVEY OF THE METHODIST PROTESTANT CHURCH

BY

LYMAN EDWYN DAVIS, D.D., LL.D.

EDITOR OF "THE METHODIST RECORDER"

NEW YORK   CHICAGO

Fleming H. Revell Company

LONDON AND EDINBURGH

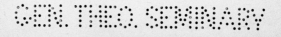

TABLE OF CONTENTS

AUTHOR'S PREFACE

THE Methodist Protestant Church, established in 1830, is a representative democracy, and its organization was a protest against the religious monarchy developed under the leadership of the early bishops of the Methodist Episcopal Church and against the autocratic manner in which that monarchy functioned in the epoch which immediately followed the signing of the Declaration of Independence.

The purpose of this topical survey is to identify, to every questioner, the various links in the chain of circumstances which led to the organization of the Methodist Protestant Church and the fundamental principles which prompted and justified the movement. Every Christian denomination that presumes to maintain a separate existence in this new day should justify itself by a real and veritable contribution to world-wide Christianity. Every separate and sovereign Church is morally bound to voice the Gospel of Christ in all its fullness, to give a clear-toned and conscientious answer to the world-wide questions of the Kingdom of God, and to prove to the Christian common sense of the world that its own distinctive principles are broad enough and vital enough to furnish a worthy complement in the sum of Christian truth, and to constitute a living factor in the progress of the Church Universal.

Can the Methodist Protestant Church justify itself in this broad and substantial way? This book is prompted and inspired by an unwavering belief in the divine mission of mutual-rights Methodism, and in the profound conviction that the continued existence of the Methodist Protestant Church, and of all churches in the Republican hemisphere of the Kingdom, is highly important to the progressive development, and even to the sure preservation, of the spirit of democracy in our American Christianity.

L. E. D.

PITTSBURGH, PA.

I

THE CORNER-STONE OF CHRISTIAN DEMOCRACY

IN every epoch of the world's history, men have reared great cities on the banks of some mighty river, and have lived and wrought there to the end of their earthly pilgrimage, some as kings and rulers, others as toilers at the humbler tasks of life, without any knowledge of the sources of that broad and kindly stream, though it nourished for them a thousand vineyards and fields, formed their only avenue of communication with other cities and nations, and carried their merchandise to the very ends of the earth. But when later travelers, each from his own proud city, have sought the headwaters of the river whose streams were sent to make them glad, they have always journeyed mountainward, finding the source of the great waters in the everlasting hills. And if they have pursued their quest in the light of the larger wisdom, they have finally learned that the clouds of heaven are the higher sources of every terrestrial river, and that even the clouds themselves are but the water-carriers of the boundless sea.

Christianity is the revelation of God to man, in the person of his only begotten Son; and the Christian Church, which is Christianity mobilized under the all-commanding authority of Jesus Christ, is commissioned to declare, as from the highest mountain-peaks of

Revelation, the spiritual Democracy upon which the Church itself is founded, and upon which, finally and forever, the civil government of the whole world must be established.

Who speaks the final word of divine authority as to the essential principles of government in Church and State? Jesus only! Jesus, who said, "All authority hath been given unto me in heaven and on earth"; Jesus, of whom it is declared, in testimony to his authority in spiritual government, that God "put all things under his feet, and gave him to be head over all things to the Church, which is his body, the fullness of him that filleth all things"; Jesus, of whom it is said, in pre-figuration of his authority over the nations, "He hath on his vesture and on his thigh a name written—King of kings, and Lord of lords!"

When we seek, in a more specific way, the Scriptural basis of church government, and hearken to the voice of Jesus with unquestioning obedience, then we hear him speak to his disciples a word of command so decisive and far-ruling that, when it is truly comprehended, it will lead to the swift banishment of every tyrant king from the realm of civil government and of every vain hierarchy from the courts of the house of God. In the eighth verse of the twenty-third chapter of Matthew we find the words which become the divine credentials of self-government for the Christian Church in all the world, and therefore the true historic justification of the Methodist Protestant Church. For, above the decrees of councils, above the voice of assemblies, convocations and conferences, above the self-constituted authorities of the ages, forever stands this final word of Jesus to his disciples of every generation: "Be ye not called rabbi, for one is your Master, even Christ; and all ye are brethren." The one supreme authority, over all, even Jesus; and his disciples forever united in an equal brotherhood of faith and service—that is the divine ideal of the Christian Church.

This Biblical standard of church government, resting as it does on the authority of the great Head of the Church, carries with it certain natural implications; and these implications are so inevitable, so vitally linked with the supremacy of Jesus, as to claim the instant obedience of every Christian. In the first place, the Saviour's injunction, by the very act of restraining his ministers from being lords over God's heritage, also restrains the people of the Christian Church from surrendering their rights to those who would become autocrats in the Lord's house. This commandment to the ministers of the Church of God becomes, by implication, a commandment of equal force and authority to every congregation of believers in Jesus Christ. The people are by this injunction forbidden to surrender the inalienable rights bequeathed unto them by the one Master of the common brotherhood of the Kingdom. And whether we look backward into the history of ancient Israel, or onward into the spirit and framework of the Apostolic Church, we find every Biblical token and suggestion arrayed against autocracy in the Church; and at every great crisis in the history of the Lord's people we hear the bugle-call of heaven in behalf of the mutual rights of the children of God. And the usages of the Church, both under the Old Dispensation and under the New Dispensation, were such as to establish the final authority of the people, under the sovereignty of Jehovah alone; so that the very election, the very anointing, of leaders among the people of God presumed and required a frequent reversion of that delegated authority to the great congregation.

The government of ancient Israel was a republican kingdom, Jehovah being the recognized sovereign, thus constituting the nation a theocracy in the one hemisphere; the people, however, enjoying the fullest measure of self-government, under divine sanction, thus constituting the nation, in the other hemisphere, a representative democracy, and making the government of Israel, through one of the most heroic periods of history, a foretype of the United States of America in the sphere of the state, and the foretype of Christian self-government in the sphere of religion. The Christian Church of the Apostolic age was a still clearer type of the spiritual republic, and every progressive revolution of the centuries, every emancipation from the bondage of oppression throughout the ages, has been at once a return to the foundations laid of old and the passionate response of the liberty-loving children of God to the challenge of the future.

The authority of Christ as the one Master in the midst of an equal brotherhood must extend, in its final radius, to every province of life, whether in Church or State. Christ is the great emancipator and the great equalizer; and he will continue the liberation of peoples and the overthrow of tyrannies until all the nations of the earth and all the churches of the kingdom of God have acknowledged his supremacy, and have entered into a world-wide fellowship of mutual service one to another, and of unquestioning loyalty to Christ. The sources of authority in a monarchy are totally different from the sources of authority in a republic. The ecclesiastical monarchy, like the political monarchy, gets authority by the artificial elevation of one man above another.   The ecclesiastical republic gets authority by exalting the majesty of the law, in the person of Jesus Christ, above the people.   The Methodist Protestant Church is a spiritual republic, forever committed to the great principle of equality in the fellowship of the kingdom.

II

HISTORIC PARALLELS

THE Protestant Reformation was threefold in its triumphal influence. First of all, it was a spiritual movement. The ecclesiastical results, while essential to the organic continuity of the Reformation, were merely outriders to the royal processional of the kingdom of God. The rise of Protestantism was simply, in its real essence, the rediscovery of the Holy Scriptures; the return of the Christian Israel from the Babylon of superstition. Following this eventful moment, there came to the Lord's anointed, on swift and holy wings, the reborn doctrine of faith, together with the accompanying grace of vital godliness in the everyday life of the disciples of Jesus. Yes, the Protestant Reformation, when carried to its logical conclusion in the lives of the people, has become a new Pentecost, enabling apostles and disciples alike to hear the oracles of the Holy Spirit.

Too often indeed, not alone in the early days of the Reformation, but in later epochs, the deeper significance of the Protestant creed has been displaced by the spirit of controversy; and, all too often, Protestant Christians have fallen into the very weaknesses which the Reformation was sent of God to overthrow. But, despite all these lapses throughout the centuries, it is forever true that the dawn of Protestantism ushered in a bright new day for the spiritual life of the whole world; it is forever true that only the Sun of Righteousness, or the morning stars that saw the glory from afar, could have revealed to the world yet again the blessed assurance that "the just shall live by faith."

The Protestant Reformation wrought changes in the intellectual world second only to those accomplished in the spiritual world. The human mind was emancipated by the Reformation, and the shackles of superstition were broken in every land which surrendered to the great movement. It may be said that the revival of learning, together with the return of independent thinking, sustained a relation of both cause and effect to the Protestant Reformation. The mind is forever holding candles for the heart; the heart is forever carrying torches for the mind. And so, in the progress of those great forces which finally issued in the Reformation as an accomplished fact, faith and learning, awakened from their age-long slumber, walked hand in hand. The Reformers themselves were scholars. Luther, Zwingli, Knox, Cranmer, Calvin—what a galaxy of learned men! And their restoration of the Bible to its place in the sanctuary as the one rule of faith and conduct, and their exaltation of the Bible as the Book of all books, opened up new and immortal springs in the field of literature. And the greatest books of three centuries were the intellectual forerunners, or else the intellectual children, of the Protestant Reformation; and all the after-literature of the nations must pay tribute to the light that dawned upon the world when Martin Luther lifted up on the temple door at Wittenberg his soul's Declaration of Independence against the corrupt tyranny of medieval Rome.

The miracle of the Protestant Reformation has found

expression also, and a never-failing testimony, in the political results of that great movement. The very genius of the Protestant Reformation, from its earliest torches in the Dark Ages to the full glory of its noonday light, is that of democracy; and the sure result of Protestant influence among the nations can be nothing short of universal liberty, with a "government of the people, for the people, and by the people." Certain oracles are seeking to lay the blame of the Great War, in some obscure way, upon the Teutonic development of the Reformation. But the spirit of Luther was the spirit of liberty. The dawn of Protestantism was simply the return of the Church to the democracy of the kingdom; and the progress of the Protestant faith signals the final overthrow of tyranny in Church and State.

The great movement known as the Protestant Reformation is an influence so constant, so constructive and beneficent as to have taken its place in the content of Christian civilization as a genuine miracle; a miracle of emancipation from the thralldom of superstition; a miracle of progress in all the highways of social and moral revolution; and a miracle of grace in the hearts of new-born millions throughout the earth.

Democratic Methodism in America, as embodied in the Methodist Protestant Church, is simply one of the projected parallels of the Reformation.

When the American Colonies, under the promptings of liberty, sent forth to the world a Declaration of Independence, and resolved themselves into a nation, they sowed the seeds of liberty and equality in every land; and the American Union has lived, not in America alone, but in the answering life and the answering hope of every liberty-loving people in the world. The battle-throb of Bunker Hill, pulsing through continents and seas, finally leveled the walls of the Bastille in Paris, and broke the shackles of ancient tyranny in a thousand citadels of power. And when religious liberty was reborn in the heart of John Huss its emancipating force was not confined to any single race or nation, but, flowing onward and outward in tidal waves of spiritual power, it permeated and influenced the future history, and in some degree determined the future destiny, of all mankind, emancipating the minds and hearts of the children of men, and flooding the Dark Ages with the glorious dawn of the Sun of Righteousness.

And in these meeting rivers of civilization, the mountain brooks of our own church history, however humble in their sources, form no inconsiderable part of the advancing stream. For what was the real meaning of that controversy which emerged in the organization of the Methodist Protestant Church? What was the larger significance of the battle-royal of the fathers in defense of the mutual rights of ministers and laymen? It was the logical sequence of Protestant history. It was the natural resultant of the two component forces of human liberty; of the political force flowing through Bunker Hill and the American Revolution, and the spiritual force, descending through all the channels of the Protestant Reformation. It was the protest of liberty-loving souls against those reactionary forces which, however harmless for the moment, were beginning to lead the world backward into the old tyrannies of Church and State.

III

THE EVOLUTION OF A CHURCH

THE great spiritual movement called Methodism crossed the Atlantic and established itself, almost simultaneously, in Maryland, and in New York, the planting process falling between 1760 and 1766; and throughout all these earliest years the leaders of the movement were true to the intensely democratic spirit of the movement.

Francis Asbury reached the New World October 27, 1771, and found himself at once in the midst of a great religious opportunity and a great political agitation. The American Colonies were stirred by the spirit of revolt, not against the Mother Country but against the Hohenzollern king who, contrary to the wiser counsels of better men, persisted in "every act which may define a tyrant." But the American Methodists of that high and tragic hour, alike in their ideals and in their moral passions, were true to the cause of the people, and autocracy, whether in Church or State, was repulsive to their every sentiment.

The group of ministers who fashioned American Methodism were themselves for the most part non-American and anti-American; the ardent friends of monarchy in Church and State; British subjects of the type of Lord North rather than of the type of William Pitt; more arbitrary in America than they would have dared to be in England itself; and so at enmity with the struggle of the American Colonies for liberty, so outspoken against the Colonists as "rebels," that when the War of the Revolution broke upon the world, they fled from the country.

Francis Asbury remained in America, but refused to take the oath of allegiance, preferring to accept asylum with friends in Delaware. But he remained not for the purpose of aiding in the slightest degree the cause of freedom and self-government in the State, but on the contrary for the purpose of developing a self-centered autocracy in the Church.

And while every Methodist Protestant will join heartily with other branches of the Christian Church in recognizing, to the most generous measuring-lines, the historic proportions of the famous leader of his people, yet no intelligent Methodist Protestant can fail to realize that Francis Asbury, more than any other figure among the pioneers of his day, is responsible for the unauthorized and unlimited powers which were bestowed upon the ministry, apart from the laity, and upon the bishops, apart from the ministry, in that epoch-making hour in Baltimore, when sixty preachers held an impromptu conference, not one layman in all Methodism being present, and placed the yoke of monarchy, for all generations, upon the neck of a democratic Church!

For Francis Asbury was not the founder of Methodism in America. Methodism came to America as a revival flame that leaped across the parting seas; and when it reached the shores of the New World it found sanctuary, not in fixed places, but in penitent human hearts. It came not as an organization, but as a pentecost; and the humblest messengers who came unsent and unsung, had more to do with the spiritual realization of

Wesley's apostolic dream than those who bore his letters of formal appointment.

But as the founder of Episcopacy, in its relation to American Methodism, Francis Asbury deserves whatsoever praise or blame may attach to that achievement. John Wesley did not appoint Mr. Coke and Mr. Asbury to be lords over God's heritage. While he himself remained a communicant of the Church of England, he realized that the War of the Revolution had made it impossible to link American Methodism with the Mother Church in the mother country. And therefore he sent special commissioners, with a message of emancipation from the English hierarchy, but not a message of subjection to a new hierarchy. He gave the American Methodists full liberty "to follow the Scriptures and the Primitive Church."

On December 25, 1784, in the city of Baltimore, under the joint direction of Mr. Coke and Mr. Asbury, supported by other notable leaders, American Methodism was clothed upon with a type of Episcopacy so inflexible as to have astonished every historian of the movement. And Bishop Asbury himself, in describing the conference, does not presume to say that Mr. Wesley had authorized or countenanced this form of organization. He made this fragmentary explanation: "It was unanimously agreed, at this conference, that circumstances made it expedient for us to become a separate body."

Arbitrary power is always cumulative in its self-assumption; and so rapid was the evolution of the Methodist hierarchy in America that even those who helped to initiate the new government began to protest against its executive severity. When a spiritual communion is organized into a hierarchy, with units of authority rising one above another, then it will surely come to pass that the tyranny exercised by the topmost unit toward the second in rank will be transmuted, with increased severity, from the second to the third, and from the third to the fourth, throughout the whole system; and all these units, by their reflex influence one upon another, must increase the rigidity of the whole ecclesiastical mechanism.

Even before the wheels of this new system were fairly on the move, however, the outcry of the people demanding a voice in the affairs of their own church began to disturb the highest authorities of the new government. And who was held chiefly responsible for the growing tyranny of Episcopal Methodism? Dr. Coke it was who, with the assistance of other elders, ordained Mr. Asbury as deacon, as elder and as superintendent, and therefore must have felt a fatherly interest in him; Dr. Coke joined with Mr. Asbury in assuming the title of bishop, without the sanction of Mr. Wesley or the Baltimore Conference, and therefore must have realized a joint responsibility with him for the overshadowing growth of the new Episcopacy. And yet, notwithstanding these mutual sympathies and responsibilities, the same Dr. Coke espoused the cause of the people as early as 1791, and although himself a bishop, thought it necessary to declare openly his "opposition to the arbitrary exercise of power by his colleague, Bishop Asbury."

The most astonishing development of the times was this surrender of American Methodists, with their new-bought liberties shining upon them, to the ecclesiastical lordship of foreign bishops, and to a form of government which British Methodists themselves had refused to accept! But this apparent submission was merely the result of the fact that the people themselves were not present at this Baltimore Conference, and had no knowledge of its proceedings. The moment they began to comprehend, then came on hurrying feet the great Snethen and his fellow reformers.

And lest it may seem that conclusions have been hastily reached in these pages, let us enter into a sympathetic survey of certain decisive events in the formative period of American Methodism, and of those incidents which are often the truest psychological mirrors of an epoch. Such a survey will disclose the evolution of an autocrat, the constitutional enthronement of a hierarchy, and the preëmption by that hierarchy of the people's every prerogative; the preëmption of every power essential to a genuine Christian democracy.

And this survey will draw upon Methodist Episcopal sources only. The testimony of the "Radicals," though altogether sufficient in itself, will be utterly discarded. The links in the narrative study of the evolution of a hierarchy form their own chain of logic and carry their own conclusions.

When Francis Asbury arrived in the New World, he found Richard Boardman shepherding the sheep of American Methodism, on the authority of John Wesley. But Mr. Asbury "saw at a glance," as one of his enthusiastic biographers declared, that Mr. Boardman was "deficient in resources and leadership." And while we are not informed as to whether Mr. Asbury reported to John Wesley this alleged incapacity of Mr. Boardman, we do know that, in the following October, a letter arrived from England authorizing Mr. Asbury to displace the man he criticized. In one short year after his promotion, however, Mr. Asbury himself was superseded by Thomas Rankin, fresh from England, and carrying the apostolic seal of the father of Methodism. Mr. Asbury's biographer once again comes to our aid with the happy assurance that Mr. Boardman accepted the promotion of his youthful colleague "in a spirit of loyalty." But it is recorded, with laudible regret, that "Rankin and Asbury were seldom able to see eye to eye." And from first to last the fact looms large, even amid his manifold labors in the Lord, that Francis Asbury very seldom found himself in agreement with any of his ecclesiastical superiors. Whether he was outranked by Boardman, Rankin, or Coke, there was no continued peace in the infant American Church until the order of precedence was reversed and he himself could hold the lash over his fellow laborers.

In 1777 a divisive question of great moment arose among the American Methodists. A majority of the preachers desired to take up the administration of the ordinances, on the ground that the Revolutionary War, with the consequent exile of their foreign ministers, had created a spiritual necessity, and therefore a providential grant of authority, for this important departure. Moreover, did they not have the illustrious example of Robert Strawbridge in thus breaking the sacramental bread to the flock that God had given to them? To that extent, indeed, they were proposing to themselves in effect an American Methodist Church established by Americans, rather than waiting for the transportation of a ready-made American Church from overseas. But Mr. Asbury was seriously and passionately opposed to the emergence of an American Methodist Church from native material. And therefore, though himself an exile among friends in Delaware, he began at once to evolve a scheme for the defeat of the "sacramental party." He realized the impossibility of accomplishing this result by direct appeal to the conference itself. He was thoroughly convinced that the next session, to be held in Fluvana County, Virginia, would determine the issue in a manner contrary to his own wishes; and this all the more surely because the Methodists of the Southern Zone, who were in favor of the administration of the ordinances, clearly outnumbered those of the Northern Zone.

How did Mr. Asbury proceed? He quietly called an ecclesiastical caucus of his own adherents in Judge White's barn in Kent County, Delaware; and that irregular conference of sixteen preachers, meeting only three weeks before the fixed date of the regular conference, quickly sensing the autocratic purpose of this meeting, proceeded to business as if they constituted the real assembly of the Church, and voted to acknowledge the authority of Asbury and to accept the appointments made by him. And the self-seeking purpose of this meeting was clearly disclosed in the fact that, while Mr. Asbury claimed to have called this group together merely to prepare them for the regular meeting, these disciples learned their real lesson so thoroughly that they remained away from the regular meeting, fully conscious of having achieved exactly what was expected of them. The regular conference met at the appointed time; but, learning of the sharp maneuver which had substituted a partisan caucus for the regular conference, resolved themselves into a presbytery, and went forth to administer the ordinances for which their people hungered.

But Francis Asbury doubtless realized that his ambition had in this instance overshot the mark, and therefore, after a psychological delay, besought the Southern "Presbytery" to discontinue the ordinances for one year, and submit the question in dispute to John Wesley. Mr. Asbury himself went from the later Northern meeting to the Southern meeting at the Brokenback church, Manakintown, Virginia, this being May 9, 1780, and made a very conciliatory address, going away nevertheless with the conviction that the conference would not accept his proposals. He retired to his lodgings, however, for a season of meditation and prayer, only returning to the conference room to bid farewell to his brethren, when he was overjoyed with the news that the conference had finally conceded all that he asked. He met this announcement with the exclamation: "Surely the hand of the Lord is in all this!"

And Mr. Asbury was sincere beyond question in his pious exclamations as in his prayers. But the spirit of the autocrat is utterly blind, even to the brightest noonday vision of Freedom and Independence; and, though unconscious of the fact, he was that day giving God the glory because these preachers had simply voted to discontinue the ordinances of the Lord's house, to discontinue the sacraments to the people that hungered for them, merely to consummate a conspiracy; they had voted to deny their people the privilege of obeying the Saviour's commandment: "Do this in remembrance of Me," that they might obey the tyrannical will of Francis Asbury.

Referring to this personal victory for Mr. Asbury in that Virginia Conference, one of his biographers unveils the whole situation to the world by two declarations. "From that hour Asbury began to be an American," says Dr. Horace M. DuBose, who also informs us in the same connection that "Asbury was now bishop de facto." Of course! And the two facts are psychologically one. Francis Asbury had refused to take the oath of allegiance throughout all the years of the War of the Revolution thus far; and both his personal journal and the conferences dominated by his influence were painfully non-committal as to the sacred cause which commanded the enthusiastic patriotism of the American people, and which had stirred even the responsive sympathy of Anglo-Saxon millions in great Britain. But now that Mr. Asbury's rivals were displaced or banished, and now that he had won the subservience of the preachers to such an extent as to have become "a de facto bishop," and is to keep up the campaign until his ambitions are fully realized, American citizenship will doubtless prove to be an asset of great value.

When the Christmas Conference of 1784 was convened in Baltimore, and Dr. Coke and his fellow-ambassadors from John Wesley had made their report to the sixty preachers in attendance, it was discovered that they did not carry with them any authority to create a bishop. Indeed both the earlier deliverances of Mr. Wesley and his later rebuke of Mr. Asbury equally evidenced his opposition to this super-Methodistic order in the ministry. His own conviction on this point was expressed in the following passage from his great historic letter to his brethren in North America: "Lord King's account of the primitive Church convinced me many years ago that bishops and presbyters are the same order, and consequently have the same right to ordain." In harmony with his conviction, Mr. Wesley did not presume to ordain Dr. Coke a bishop; and therefore Dr. Coke could not have ordained Francis Asbury a bishop. And the members of the Christmas Conference at Baltimore, ready as they were to forward the wishes of their leaders, did not presume to elect either Mr. Coke or Mr. Asbury to any office other than the general superintendency to which Wesley had commissioned them.

But, as already indicated, the title of bishop was assumed through an ad interim decision or process of which there is no record. And if there are those who presume to make light of the difference between these two words, the passionate way in which the title of bishop is at once sought by the self-seeker and opposed by the spirit of democracy, is in itself enough to prove that the two words, in their psychological appeal, are as far apart as the east is from the west. The etymology of the word bishop is indeed as innocent of tyranny as a shepherd's crook; but the historic content of the word, as acquired through the ecclesiastical adjustments of the ages, visualizes to the common sense of the world the autocrat rather than the minister, and becomes to the lips of ambition sweeter than honey and the honey-comb.

As soon as the lash was well in hand, and the autocrat had enough fellow-rulers to form a hierarchy, three great progressive demands arose among the preachers and the people. First of all came the right of appeal, followed by the immediate and finally successful overthrow of the right of appeal. In the General Conference of 1792, Rev. James O'Kelley introduced the following:

"Resolved, That after the bishop appoints the preachers at conference to their several circuits, if any one thinks himself injured by the appointment, he shall have liberty to appeal to the conference and state his objections; and, if the conference approve his objections, the bishop shall appoint him to another circuit."

Such a resolution rests of course upon the very foundations of Democracy, whether in Church or State, and every reader in America would intuitively expect to hear that the resolution was passed without opposition. But the hierarchy was opposed to this reasonable concession, and it was actually defeated. James O'Kelley, however, left the Methodist Episcopal Church because of a decision so repulsive to the citizens of a Republic, and thousands of members joined him in this memorable departure. In our Methodist Protestant Church this right of appeal from the appointing power of the conference is of course a reciprocal right, as between the ministry and the laity, each lay-delegate having the right of appeal to the open conference on behalf of his church, while the itinerant enjoys this right on his own behalf. But the right of appeal thus denied more than a century ago is still denied to the ministers of the Methodist Episcopal Church; and, as Nicholas Snethen aptly says, "the bishop has every traveling preacher on the tip of his pen, and he can write him wherever he will."

When King John and the barons of England met at Runnymede, the principle of human rights received very much broader recognition than in the Baltimore General Conference of 1792. The people were indeed absent from the great historic event at Runnymede; but the barons won from the tyrant king a Magna Charta, which, however slow the process, finally filtered out among the people. The bishops at Baltimore, in their opposition to the right of appeal, were as autocratic as King John;

and the preachers, who had joined with the bishops in excluding the people, were the ecclesiastical barons of the hour. But even these ecclesiastical barons failed to get a Magna Charta! The hierarchy had preëmpted every sovereign function, whether it belonged of right to the ministers or to the people!

One of the burning questions of the epoch of controversy was that which concerned the Presiding Elders of the Methodist Episcopal Church. The bishops from the beginning had appointed the Presiding Elders, without either the advice or consent of the Annual Conference. An agitation in favor of the election of the Presiding Elders by the Annual Conference arose very soon after the organization of the Church. In the General Conference of 1808 this question was prominently brought to the front, a resolution being offered for the election of the Presiding Elders by the Annual Conference, but the outcome of this debate was the ultimate defeat of the proposition, and the Episcopal appointment of Presiding Elders, together with all that belonged to the Episcopacy at that time, was held to have found shelter under the Constitution.

This question of the election of the presiding elders by the conference was so keenly divisive that the vote in several instances was very close, the majority against the Reformers in 1812 being only three. But the constitutional battle in this twenty years' war was fought in 1808. Bishop Thomas B. Neely, in his book entitled, "The Bishops and the Supervisional System," designates those who fought for the election of Presiding Elders by the conference as "innovators," and proceeds to suggest their motive in these words: "It was important, therefore, for these innovators to get their proposition considered and adopted before the adoption of the Constitution. If they could secure the adoption of an elective presiding eldership by the existing General Conference, then the delegated General Conference, with its restricted powers, would not, by itself, be able to change it."

Bishop Neely in his every book that bears upon the Mutual-Rights controversy has been eminently fair with the Methodist Protestants; but in this instance the logic of the situation is contrary to the implications that run with his statement of the presiding-eldership case in 1808. The official advantage in the controversy was certainly enjoyed by the bishops, who had the whip-hand upon every intinerant, from the power of promotion and demotion to the practical question of bread and butter for the parsonage. And, moreover, the sequel of the whole discussion, as disclosed twelve years later, was something more than a mere guess on the subject of master-motives. For in 1820 the bishops made a wall of technicality against every tidal-wave of conference sentiment; and even a majority of more than two-thirds was finally beaten down by the plea that the proposed change was unconstitutional. Every succeeding link in the chain of events from the arrival of Asbury to the adoption of a constitution of the Methodist Episcopal Church in 1808, becomes additional and cumulative evidence of the fact that the bishops themselves, and not the mutual-rights reformers, were the "innovators" in the evolution of American Methodism; innovators, first of all, because of the self-seeking maneuvers by which personal ambition finally quenched the spirit of democracy in the new Church, and innovators to the last, in that they assumed the title of an office to which they were not elected even by subservient preachers of 1784, and which they constantly and persistently developed into an unlimited monarchy of the most exclusive type. And, therefore, the motive which Bishop Neely imputes to the tribunes of democracy in the General Conference of 1808 is imputed by the logic of the situation to those who occupied the seats of power; and history itself requires the reversal of Bishop Neely's statement; requires that it should be put in this form: "The bishops knew that if they could lodge in the Constitution their power to appoint the Presiding Elders, without either the advice or consent of the conference, they would be forever able to ignore the champions of self-government."

The question so persisted, however, despite the presumed constitutional settlement of it, that in the General Conference of 1820, a compromise resolution was offered providing that the bishops should nominate three times the number of Presiding Elders required, and that from these nominees the conference should elect; and this resolution was carried by a vote of sixty-one to twenty-five.

Then the hierarchy began to function at once through the initiative of Joshua Soule, a bishop-elect, who excused himself from the conference the moment the vote was declared; and through the next few hours that followed his withdrawal, busied himself with the preparation of a remarkable letter, addressed not to the conference, which was the voting body, but to the bishops themselves. In this message, Mr. Soule said: "I cannot consistently with my convictions of propriety and obligation, enter upon the work of an itinerant General Superintendent. I was elected under the constitution and Government of the Methodist Episcopal Church unimpaired."

This letter, after having been considered in long sittings by the bishops themselves, was finally reported to the General Conference, accompanied by the cautious but unyielding endorsement of all the bishops save one. And the attitude of the bishops, aided by the vigorous campaigning of their lieutenants, finally wrought sufficient influence to enable the Episcopal party to pass a noncommittal motion to the effect that the rule passed in favor of the election of presiding elders be suspended until the next Conference; and, at the next General Conference, six of the annual conferences having in the interim supported the cause of the bishops, while conferences such as the New York and the Baltimore declined to vote, it was declared that the resolutions passed by a vote of more than two to one were "not of authority, and shall not be carried into effect."

In a word, the General Conference of 1820 was literally held up by the hierarchy. It was perhaps the most eventful ecclesiastical hold-up in the history of modern Christianity!

But the controlling spirit of this great question was foreshadowed in the General Conference of 1812; and the one incident in that conference, an incident of the type which often mirrors a whole epoch, is put forth here as an all-sufficient content of the whole controversy of that day between American Methodists and their self-constituted bishops.

This incident finds description in an article which appeared in the "Zion's Herald" of April 3, 1876. The paragraph covering this subject is as follows:

"It is gratifying to those New Englanders who are now contending for the election of Presiding Elders, to know that Jesse Lee, their apostle, was a determined advocate of that just and essentially conservative measure of reform. He contended for it boldly, especially on the floor of the General Conference of 1812, when Bishop Asbury, to show his dislike of the measure, with unpardonable discourtesy, turned his back upon the speaker —sitting with his back to the Conference. Some charged Lee with a lack of common sense; whereupon he rose and said, 'Mr. President, Brother ——— has said that no man of common sense would use such arguments as I did. . . . I am, therefore, compelled to believe the brother thinks me a man of uncommon sense.' 'Yes, yes,' said Asbury, turning half round in his chair, 'yes, yes, Brother Lee, you are a man of uncommon sense.' 'Then sir,' rejoined the ready-witted Lee, 'I beg that uncommon attention may be paid to what I am about to say.' This retort, which contained a but half-concealed rebuke of the Bishop's discourteous conduct, provoked a smile throughout the Conference, but did not prevent the continuance of the Bishop's rudeness; for, says Leroy M. Lee, he resumed 'his face to the wall position.'"

The pitiful situation thus portrayed by "Zion's Herald," the great New England organ of the Methodist Episcopal Church, is a true mirror of the epoch to which it belongs; a genuine content of the kind of tyranny which prevailed over the spirit of Democratic Methodism in America during the controversy out of which emerged the Methodist Protestant Church. The evolution of a hierarchy in the one church, became through opposing forces in the same process, the evolution of another church.

And now that the hierarchy had made the Presiding Elder an appointee of the Bishop, in perpetuity, and had silenced every voice that claimed the right of appeal from arbitrary pastoral appointments, it was only a short step to the unyielding denial of the mutual rights of the ministry and the laity. The presiding eldership question was side-tracked in 1820, and finally cast out in 1824; and this same General Conference of 1824, witnessed the decisive action of the hierarchy against the claims of the laity to any share in the government of the Church.

The deliverance of the autocrats on this question was indeed so coldly final and uncompromising as to indicate a vain sense of irresponsible power. "Pardon us," they said, "if we know no such rights, if we comprehend no such privileges." And the inquisition which from that hour was launched with renewed energy against the Reformers, gave ample evidence of the fact that the members of the hierarchy "comprehended no such privileges"; that they comprehended only such a procedure as would forever enthrone the Monarchy in American Methodism, and forever dispossess the people. Ministers and laymen alike were forbidden even to read the "Mutual Rights," and other literature devoted to representative Church government, though the ablest pens of the Methodism of that day were dedicated to the good cause. And, when both ministers and laymen persisted in exercising that freedom of speech, and in upholding that freedom of the press which is fundamental to democracy in Church and State alike, groups of Reformers in Baltimore, Cincinnati and other cities were expelled from the Methodist Episcopal Church, these martyrs to the cause of freedom and self-government being, on the unanimous testimony of friends and persecutors alike, Christians of the most exemplary kind, against whose moral character not one whisper was abroad. And when two of the expelled champions of reform, Dennis B. Dorsey and William C. Pool, appealed their case to the

General Conference of the Methodist Episcopal Church, which met in Pittsburgh in 1828, the act of expulsion was finally sustained, notwithstanding the unrighteousness of the act itself, and despite the irregular, illegal and unjust procedure by which the act was consummated.

One incident in the hearing of the Pool-Dorsey appeal by the General Conference of 1828, is so very interesting as to compete with the event itself. After the action of the Baltimore Conference had been sustained, and the expulsion of the two reformers had been thus confirmed, a supplementary resolution was passed to the effect that the action should not be interpreted as in any manner an infringement of the freedom of speech, or the freedom of the press, in the Methodist Episcopal Church; and severely condemning, by anticipation, any one who should dare to arrive at such a conclusion. This resolution simply proved, in its ultimate psychology, not the truth of what was proclaimed in the resolution, but the official consciousness of the fact that it was not true; and it forms one of the most humorous incidents of ecclesiastical history. This supplementary, self-defensive protestation would be truly embodied in this form:

Resolved, That we hereby endorse, seal and consummate the expulsion of these appellants, for no other reason than that they have merely exercised that liberty of speech and of the press which is guaranteed to American citizens of every creed and of every party.

Resolved, That we nevertheless continue to recognize and proclaim liberty of speech and of the press as being ·fundamental to a free people, whether in Church or State.

Resolved, finally, That we call upon all men everywhere to interpret the excommunication of these worthy brethren, as being in no wise an infringement of the liberty of speech or of the press.

No wonder the great leaders of that day, whether they later affiliated with the Methodist Episcopal Church or the Methodist Protestant Church, voiced their passionate indignation against the cumulative tyranny of these *"lords over God's heritage!"* No wonder that those who were later whipped in by the hierarchy protested just as vigorously as those who were whipped out! No wonder that Henry B. Bascom, though himself a bishop in after years, denounced this act of excommunication as "an overbearing act of abandoned infamy!" No wonder that William McKendree, though destined to equal prominence in the future history of Episcopal Methodism called the denial of the right of appeal an insult "to his understanding!" No wonder the "Catholic Telegraph" of Cincinnati declared that the Catholic Church never set up a higher claim to power than the Methodist Episcopal deliverance of 1828!

IV

AN AMERICAN BILL OF RIGHTS

IN the evolution of the Methodist Protestant Church certain definite principles emerged; and with every event in the epoch of organization, these principles loomed larger still, until they became a well-rounded creed of liberty and self-government, lifting democratic Methodism above the realm of controversy and giving it a sacred mission among the churches of Christ in America.

The first article in the creed of self-government as developed by the founders of the Methodist Protestant Church is that of mutual rights; this now historic phrase signifying an equal voice by the ministry and the laity of the Church in all conferences and congregations. This ecclesiastical doctrine is not the outgrowth of radical opinion. It is an orthodox principle of Christianity, breathing the very spirit of the gospel, and reposing, deep-laid, in the very foundations of the Church, close to the rock Christ Jesus. The Methodist Protestant Church has been true to this vital and fundamental principle from first to last; and the virtue of this fidelity lies not in the mere fact of it; not in the mere record of conformity with the creed of the fathers; but rather in the passionate conviction that the mutual rights of the ministry and the laity is the keystone of true democracy in the kingdom of Christ, and that the founders of the Methodist Protestant Church, by giving to this principle the place of honor in their creed of self-govern-

ment, have made a permanent contribution to the cause
of religious liberty throughout the earth.

The principle of mutual rights, as between the ministry
and the laity, was of course not new to the world in the
epoch which led to the organization of the Methodist
Protestant Church. That principle lies at the very root
of Christian democracy in every generation, and the
great historic departures of the people from the priest-
craft of the Dark Ages was simply the revival of this
elementary doctrine in the creed of human rights. The
glory of Snethen and his fellow reformers is simply this:
that they responded to the battle call of religious freedom in their own day as truly, as valiantly and as wisely
as did John Huss in Bohemia, John Knox in Scotland
and John Robinson in England; and that their warfare
against the encroachments of a Methodist hierarchy in
America, a hierarchy unauthorized by the voice of the
people, has led not only to the forming of the Methodist
Protestant Church as the organic expression of democratic Methodism, but also to the slow-moving and re-
luctant recognition, and yet to the progressive and hopeful recognition, of this same essential of liberty within
the domains of the still prevailing monarchy of the
Methodist Episcopal Church.

In the creed of Christian democracy, as adopted by the
Methodist Protestant Church, individual rights are as
jealously guarded as are the mutual rights of the ministers and members. These personal rights are proclaimed and guarded by the constitution of the Methodist Protestant Church in three provinces of ecclesiastical life. Superadded to the right of petition, which
is common to all the zones of self-government in Church
and State alike, our fathers wisely magnified the right

of appeal. And this right of appeal, while applying to
every field of jurisprudence and to every individual case,
becomes one of the crown-jewels of democratic Methodism in its application to the appointing power of the
annual conference. For whatever the agency through
which pastoral assignments are made by the annual conference of the Methodist Protestant Church, the ultimate authority rests with the whole conference in open
session, the ministry and laity being equally represented;
and every minister dissatisfied with his appointment has
the right of appeal on his own behalf to the whole conference, and the lay delegate representing any one of the
constituent churches has the same inalienable right. In
either case, the appointment in question goes back to
the appointing agency without debate, and with the comforting knowledge of the fact that the whole conference
has continual veto power and the power of final decision. And the history of our denomination would disclose many a dramatic moment on the floor of every
annual conference, when every member of the body,
minister and layman alike, had reason to thank God for
the liberty-loving vision of the fathers as manifested in
the declaration and the safeguarding of this constitutional right of appeal.

Occupying a high and glorious place among the individual rights guaranteed to the ministers and members
of the Methodist Protestant Church is "the right to private judgment in matters of religion." The zone of
essential doctrine is clearly defined in the constitution
of the Methodist Protestant Church, and the Holy Bible
is the "only sufficient rule of faith and practice." But
within the broad and high circumference of things im-
movable and eternal; within the divine circle of things

beyond doubt or question, democratic Methodism in America leaves the human mind unfettered and unswaddled; and along with the right to private judgment goes also emancipated types and emancipated tongues; for it is clearly provided that "no rule shall be passed which shall infringe the liberty of speech or of the press." And, once upon a time, when a whole General Conference was in imminent danger of forgetting this fundamental right, a famous tribune of the people found it only necessary to quote this one great article from the Magna Charta of liberal Methodism.

The third quadrant of the circle of self-government in the Methodist Protestant Church is given to the safeguarding of the equal status of the ministers of the gospel. Democratic Methodism in America recognizes but one order in the ministry: and "all elders in the Church of God are equal."

This article is based upon the Scriptural injunction which forbids ministers of the gospel to be lords over God's heritage; and the evolution of events, both in Church and State, has been an ever-increasing justification of the fidelity of our fathers to this great principle.

The great charter of democratic Methodism in America includes, last of all, but not least of all, a provision which forever safeguards the constitutional liberties of the whole denomination.

The mutual rights of the ministry and the laity; the individual rights of all, whether ministers or members; the equal rights of all the ministers, determined and secured by their equal status under the one and only order; and, finally, the proclaimed and fortified liberties of the whole people, the whole Church—these are the four quadrants of the circle of freedom and self-government in the Methodist Protestant Church.

And how is this all-important realm of democratic Methodism secured? Here are the last words of the "elementary principles," the bill of rights, the Magna Charta, of the Methodist Protestant Church: "But she—the Church—has no right to create any distinct or independent sovereignties."

In a word, the founders of democratic Methodism in America were so gifted with the very genius of liberty that they foresaw the possible destruction of equal-rights Methodism through the delegated or assumed powers of men, or groups of men, who were but the subordinates and creatures of the Church in General Conference assembled.

In a word, the government of the Methodist Protestant Church rests upon a four-cornered foundation of inalienable Christian rights: The right of appeal from the subordinate and transitory agents of authority to the representative sources of authority; the right of every American assembly, whether civil or ecclesiastical, to choose its own leader; the co-equal rights of the ministry and the laity in every legislative body of the Church; the right of every man, within the bounds of faith and loyalty, to think for himself, and to exercise that liberty of speech which is altogether essential to self-government, whether in Church or State; and, as a corollary to these hallowed principles, the sovereign right of a denomination to safeguard its fundamental principles from treason within as well as from assault without.

In connection with this American bill of rights, it is important to realize that the principles involved therein constitute a present-day issue, pressing for recognition at every door. The rights comprehended in this creed of religious liberty are still in jeopardy, in Church and State alike, and are in need of ardent and sincere defenders in every arena. The right of appeal, the right to representation in governing bodies, the right of conferences and congregations to elect their own leaders, every right that finds analogy in the government of our country is as thoroughly disregarded to-day by the autocratic rulers of the Methodist Episcopal Church as they were in the days of our fathers ninety years ago; and while a refined diplomacy now softens the fiat of the ruling powers, they are still saying, through their Episcopal functions at the Annual Conference:

"Pardon us if we comprehend no such rights and privileges."

It has been said by the advocates of Episcopacy that the bishops of to-day are not like those of an hundred years ago, and that while modern bishops still hold the scepter of unlimited power, they do not exercise that power in its fulness; and of course by the implications of this argument we are bidden to grant unlimited authority to Christian leaders in the confident hope that they may not be disposed to over-exercise authority. But let the apologists suggest that method of procedure to London or Washington. Let them say to Great Britain:

"King George is a ruler of noble and kindly disposition, and both his convictions and his sympathies are with the people. Therefore, clothe him with the kingly prerogatives of your ancient rulers!"

Or say to the American nation:

"Your president is so entirely a man of the multitude, so pervaded and dominated by the spirit of democracy that he could safely be entrusted with the prerogatives of a king!"

But Anglo-Saxon history in every epoch has proven that the safety of popular government, and even the very life of human liberty, depends upon permanent constitutional provisions against tyranny, whether the ruler of to-day may chance to be a Caligula or a Victoria. And the Constitution of the United States is but the ripened harvest of Anglo-Saxon experience.

The founders of the Methodist Protestant Church, building perhaps even better than they knew, framed an American Bill of Rights which forever safeguards the sacred principles for which they contended. And the organization of the Church answers true to its elementary principles. On the one hand the legislative and judiciary functions are lodged in the General Conference; and this highest court of the Church becomes in itself the embodiment of supreme authority, sending abroad to the Annual Conferences the laws and policies which are to obtain throughout the Church. And in these Annual Conferences, rather than in any super-official above the conferences, are lodged the executive and administrative functions of the denomination, together with the right to pass such rules and regulations of their own as do not conflict with the supreme law of the General Conference.

To the Annual Conference president is given, for administrative reasons, a greater degree of immediate authority than is lodged in any other official of the Methodist Protestant Church; for he has the power to release pastors and to appoint pastors ad interim. But so wisely cautious were the founders of our Church that they linked even these temporary powers with the inalienable rights of the local Church, providing that the president may release or appoint only in conjunction with the quarterly conference. Thus a safe stable equilibrium is assured between the two hemispheres of our denominational government, and at the same time the limited powers bestowed are fairly distributed throughout the territory of the Church, promising to insure to our communion, when these wise provisions are fully understood, that mutual confidence and coöperation which makes a republic the most efficient form of government known to Church or State.

At this high moment in the progress of world-wide Methodism the two divergent forms of Church government have become two diverging forces. The Methodism of Great Britain is non-Episcopal and the Methodism of Canada is non-Episcopal; and in the recent movement leading to Church union in the Dominion of Canada, even though the Methodist Episcopal Church itself was included in the union, the resultant organization, the Methodist Church of Canada, emerged from the crucible in non-Episcopal form.

This fact is deeply significant, if not prophetic; and though the Methodist Protestant Church as a unit of democratic methodism in America is overshadowed by the larger bodies of Episcopal Methodism, she has no reason to fear the future, much less to turn aside from the high mission to which she has been called. The opportunity of democratic Methodism in America is now at hand and conditions throughout the world, in Church and State alike, are favorable to her long cherished ideals.

V

ORGANIC EFFICIENCY OF SELF-GOVERNMENT

THE Christian Church of the future, if it is to become the glorious Church for which the Christ is longing, must be the constant and courageous defender of freedom and self-government, both in Church and State. Liberty is the commanding citadel of civilization, and to surrender that fortress is to surrender all. And yet there is a growing temptation to sacrifice freedom to bondage, self-government to autocracy, the life to the organization, the man to the machine. This tendency grows out of the passion for outward efficiency. Of course nobody wants the tyranny of the autocrat nor the tyranny of the organization; but if the autocrat or the organization can get things done, if the greatest achievement can be accomplished in the least possible time, if only the harvest of success can be reaped from the fields of oppression, then the tyrant becomes a hero in this age of ours, and the organization becomes a god.

Even when this tolerance of the tyrant is driven from the political world, it finds a safe retreat in the realm of religion; because, in the dearth of spiritual vision, men do not take account of religious liberty or of religious oppression. If the body feels the lash, then the freeman rises in all the majesty of manhood and rebels against the tyrant that wields the lash. If a nation is so reduced to servitude that the whole body politic is under the tyrant's thumb, and the whole multitude of the people must do a tyrant's bidding, even unto shame and death, then a William Tell springs forth from every mountain cradle of liberty. When a new continent is threatened with political servitude, then a Washington is given to the people. But so insinuating, so elusory, so imperceptible to the common eye are the encroachments of religious oppression and tyranny that a thousand years of cumulative darkness may overspread the world before a John Huss and his kindred moral heroes come forth to emancipate the captive nations of the earth.

But we must finally learn, and we must forever remember, that religious liberty is the very soul of civil liberty; that religious liberty begins with the emancipation of the soul from the bondage of darkness, by the power of the living God, through Jesus Christ the liberator of all mankind, and that therefore religious liberty is the one perennial spring that nourishes all the gardens of freedom in all the earth. In the background of every national surrender to the political tyrant looms the moral surrender of God's people to the religious tyrant. Back of the Romanoffs, the Hapsburgs and the Hohenzollerns lurks that subtile fallacy called the divine right of kings; and that fallacy is simply the badge of a religious tyranny which antedates, anoints and confirms the political tyrant. Man's relation to the supernatural is the source of his earliest dreams, his primal thoughts, his master motives and his eternal hopes; and, whatsoever the creed of the man, or whatsoever his vain denial of all the creeds, the religion of mankind dominates the political philosophy of mankind. Every would-be tyrant of the ages, intuitively knowing this, strives to plant his despotism in the soil of faith; and that convenient phrase, "the divine right of kings," is interpreted by the tyrant as giving him the right to lash the people, to enthrall the nation, and to crush the heart of freedom in every land.

The analogy between civil liberty and religious liberty is clearly revealed to all the world by the events and consequences of the last great war. The leaders of every nation, even the leaders of the Anglo-Saxon world, paid high tribute to the latest German emperor, so long as he kept the peace; so long as his tightening of the chains of military slavery and his building of the war machine for world conquest was unaccompanied with the awful advent of war. The world then applauded the grand efficiency of that military lock-step to which every form of life was mustered in the Central Empires. How fine it was to have every human activity go forward with the precision of a perfect timepiece! How glorious to see a whole nation mark time and keep step, like well-drilled soldiers, even when going to school, even when going to work! And in that epoch of awful preparation, even a Carnegie, even a Roosevelt, extolled the virtues and saw not the dangers of the last of the Hohenzollerns. But when the storm of battle broke upon a sleeping world, then the liberty-loving nations of the earth, after standing palsied and aghast for one high and decisive moment, flew to arms, comprehending at last that mere efficiency, mere success, mere achievement, though imperial and world-wide in its glittering triumph, may hide within itself the very fires of hell. And, resolving that, rather than sacrifice liberty to efficiency, outward efficiency itself, if need be, should be sacrificed to liberty; and resolving, also, by the grace of the living God, to witness to all the world that freedom is ultimately more efficient than tyranny, and that a self-governing people are finally more efficient, through vital union and moral initiative, than any tyrant-ruled people can ever become through the slavish discipline of the military camp. And on the broadest battlefields of history, Great Britain, France and America, aided by the new-born peoples of the earth, have given final evidence of the fact that while free and self-ruling nations may not be as ready for war as the nations that bow to the over-government of the autocrats, yet when these liberty-loving peoples are awakened by the battle call of freedom, and are thrilled and united by the love of humanity, their organic energy, and therefore their final efficiency, is equal to the overthrow of all the hosts of tyranny. All the battle monuments of history witness this truth to the heavens and the earth; the battle monuments of the ancient world, from Marathon to Chalons; all the battle monuments of the modern world, from Bunker Hill to Waterloo, and from Waterloo to Verdun and Ypres, the Marne and the Argonne.

The Methodist Protestant Church, by all the alignments of her history, as well as by her unchanging principles, is arrayed on the side of freedom and self-government, as against every form of despotism. Representing democratic Methodism in America, and restoring in their polity the well-known ideals of John Wesley, Methodist Protestants claim a share in the government of their church, as well as a share in the government of their country. And they are convinced that, in Church and State alike, freedom and equality before the law are the unfailing essentials of real progress. Notwithstanding the cruel lessons of the Great War, however, there is still a passion for bulk and bigness. But if liberty is second to bulk and bigness, then the ancient

Greeks should have surrendered Thermopylæ and Marathon to the hordes of the Persian tyrant, and the America of George Washington should have hauled down her flag to the German tyrant who for a time occupied the throne of England. If freedom and self-government are secondary to bulk and bigness, then should democratic Methodism in America cease to live, and the Protestant Churches of the world should surrender to the Roman Catholic hierarchy; and, inasmuch as Christians are still outnumbered by non-Christians throughout the earth, the Christian Church should call back her missionaries and surrender the whole world to the pagans!

VI

NEWBORN REPUBLICS ON PROBATION

THE great war, with all its furies, was brought upon the world by the autocrats of Central Europe, and therefore, as the natural and inevitable consequence of freedom's victory, the autocrats responsible for the awful carnage were overthrown, and republics sprang into being from every territory formerly ruled by the tyrants. Certain countries were doubtless ripe for revolution and certain peoples were truly hungry for self-government; and in such regions the spirit of democracy promises to be an abiding presence and a permanent ruling power. But history teaches us, through a thousand oracles, that revolution invites counter-revolution, and that, whether in Church or State, newborn republics must always serve a period of probation.

In the realm of civil government, yonder in Central Europe, this probationary state is plainly manifest, at this hour, to all the world. The present situation in Germany discloses indeed a twofold probation. The new German republic is clearly on probation, first of all, to the German people themselves. There are millions of Germans who already long for the restoration of the monarchy, and, pervading the whole superstructure of the republican government, refluent in the very life-blood of the new democracy, there is a returning spirit of allegiance to the Hohenzollerns. This haunting presence of the ancient monarchy in the house of the new re-

public fills all the land with doubt, so that even the
staunchest friends of the new order, even the very
leaders of the new government, realize that Germany's
newborn republic is but a vast experiment; that the Germany of to-day is on probation to the Germany of yesterday, and that, in any nation-wide crisis, this modern
structure might prove as frail as a house of cards.

But if the newborn republic of Germany is on probation to Germany herself, how much more seriously must
that republic serve a period of probation to the world-
wide spirit of democracy, and to the firmly established
republics of Europe and America! For everybody knows
that when a republic is proclaimed in a land which has
never known any form of government save only the rule
of the tyrants, that land will long possess, not alone the
secretly organized agents of the fallen dynasty, supported
by innumerable sympathizers among the people, but, most
significant of all, a monarchial temperament; an all-
pervading national spirit which fails to comprehend
democracy; a spirit which has taught the people, through
the mental habits of the ages, to attune themselves to
the will of a king; a spirit which has transmuted even
patriotism into hero-worship, and hero-worship into
king-worship. The conditions which now prevail in
Germany are but a repetition of like conditions in every
country which has passed, either transiently or perma-
nently, from the valley of oppression to the mount of
freedom. The democracy of the British people is an
evolution of the centuries. And who can measure the
depths of woe through which our Anglo-Saxon mother-
land has passed in her long journey to the light and liberty of the Victorian age? And as for France, the land
of Lafayette, it required almost one hundred years for

that great nation to develop the spasmodic freedom of the Revolution into the established liberty of the age of Clemenceau.

And what conclusion must we draw from the logic of history? We are forced to conclude that, just as the spirit of democracy could not have safely intrusted herself to the ephemeral republics of the past, so the spirit of democracy to-day must put every newborn republic on probation, refusing her final seal of approval and recognition until the victory of freedom in the lands so lately emancipated from tyranny has been consolidated. Even if the established republic of Switzerland bordered directly upon Germany, and even though all her people spoke the German language, it would endanger the freedom and independence of Switzerland to permit herself to be absorbed with the untried German republic; and such a step could not be safely taken until generations of progressive development have brought Germany to the same unwavering love of liberty and self-government which now prevails in America and in the hearts of our allies across the sea.

Answering to the tumult of the people, and as a natural and inevitable aftermath to the overthrow of the political tyrannies of Europe, there is now in all the world a noble and irresistible passion for the organization of republics. And this democratic tidal wave has swept across the religious world, until denominations which hitherto, in all their history, have excluded the laity from any substantial share in the government of the Church, are now hastening to readjust their polity and bring it into working harmony with the new era. A joint commission, representing the Methodist Episcopal Church and the Methodist Episcopal Church,

South, have recently adopted a general basis of union;
and, while this is of course subject to the action of the
two general conferences, and must then go as an overture to the annual conferences of both denominations,
and secure the ratification of two-thirds of these conferences, the whole Christian world will rejoice in the consummation of such a union.

But even if these two great churches should become
the one greater Church, and even if the United Church,
under the spell of the new democracy, should adopt a
republican form of government, it is still true, in Church
and State alike, that the newborn republic must of necessity pass through an experimental stage; and in the
eyes of those who, from the very beginning, despite per-
secutions innumerable, have always stood for democratic Methodism in America, any ecclesiastical republic
which suddenly emerges from a century of unlimited
monarchy is to be encouraged as a noble venture, but not
to be at once accepted as a final, and permanent consummation.

The ultimate germ of autocracy is to be found, not
in the individual ruler, but primarily in those constitutional laws and precedents that open wide the doors of
opportunity to the tyrant; and therefore England made
her great unwritten constitution so democratic as to insure self-government to her people at all times, with
equal certainty, whether under a mild ruler of the democratic house of Windsor, or in the possible emergence
of a ruler of the type of the ancient Stuarts or
Plantagenets. But the germ of autocracy is also hid-
den, under the shadow of every newborn republic, in
the constant activity of the autocratic forces that hitherto
occupied the seats of power. It follows clearly, there-

fore, that, both for their own safety and for the cause of freedom and self-government throughout the world, every long-established republic, whether in Church or State, should faithfully maintain her identity until this experimental epoch is surely past. And, just as little Switzerland or big America will best encourage the new-born republics of political Europe by keeping their flags lifted high and their own trumpets sounding afar, so the established republics of the kingdom of Christ, whether numerically great or small, will most surely and effectively encourage every noble experiment in self-government by standing fast in the liberty wherewith Christ hath made them free.

ROLL-CALL OF THE FATHERS

WHEN a new denomination of Christians is organized for the distinct purpose of re-establishing and preserving some forgotten principle of the Christian faith, that principle becomes a sacred and perpetual heritage. The leaders of every epoch in such a church are therefore at once the children of the past and the fathers of the future; builders with God upon the foundations laid of old, and yet re-founders of the Church, in that they lay, broader and deeper still, the corner-stones of the faith for future generations; seekers indeed after the Old Paths, and yet the heroic pioneers of the "new and living way."

Who were the Fathers of the Methodist Protestant Church? If we were required to name our denominational founders, in the broadest and deepest sense, we should be compelled to call the roll of the faithful in every community that received the hand-planting of Liberal Methodism. The real and epic struggles of the Christian world in behalf of religious liberty, and therefore the supreme heroisms of the Faith, are associated, not with General Conferences and General Assemblies alone, but very often, in a most vital way, with local congregations in quiet neighborhoods, where new-sown principles must find congenial soil and steadfast cultivation, and where they must grow up despite the buffeting of every wind that blows, until they finally

compel recognition as a part of the world-wide vineyards of the Lord. If, therefore, you would enroll the
ultimate founders of the Methodist Protestant Church,
then must you visit a thousand churchyards, covering
all the wide fields of labor traveled by the Fathers, and
from the witnessing monuments of each community
that received the glorious ministry of long ago, transcribe
the humble but hallowed names of all the myriads who
fought for us the good fight and left to us the legacy
of their achievements.

But the first generation of disciples in the field of
Mutual Rights clearly recognized certain leaders as the
apostles of the movement, and history has confirmed this
judgment by honoring and recording these men as the
forefathers and founders of the Methodist Protestant
Church. At the head of this roll of honor stands unchallenged the name of Nicholas Snethen. And this
primacy belongs to Snethen, not by the artificial elevation of one man above another, not by a mere majority
vote in a contest between rival favorites, not by any
badge of distinction separating him from the common
lot of his brethren; but simply because of his heaven-
born genius for persuasive leadership, because of his
equal proficiency in the knowledge of books and of men,
because of his well-poised and noble character, because
of his sincere and thorough devotion to the rights of
the people, and, above all else, because these lofty human
qualities were enriched and crowned with an unfailing
faith in God and in the final triumph of liberty in every
province of the Kingdom of Christ.

Snethen's priority among the Fathers is still further
established by the wide range of his gracious and fruitful ministry. Other itinerants traveled their circuits

great and small, and their life-time service often included many charges, making every man of them a "Prophet of the long road." But Nicholas Snethen wrought his noble achievements in so many forms of service and sowed the good seed of the Kingdom in so many quarters of the land, that the whole country was his parish. Born on Long Island in 1769, he died in 1845 in the midst of a journey to Iowa City, where he was to assume the presidency of the "Snethen School for Young Ministers." And how can we glimpse, in one brief moment, the seventy-five years of that eventful life? Opening the windows of the past, and looking backward along the highway of the Fathers, we behold Nicholas Snethen, fulfilling his calm and noble career, now proving his call to the ministry with five toilsome and fruitful years among the hills of New England; now feeding the flock of God with equal wisdom and fidelity, in the metropolis of the New World; now the traveling companion of Bishop Asbury, himself often filling Mr. Asbury's place, to the delight of the people, whether as a preacher in the pulpit or as a presiding officer in the annual conference; now waging a great battle for mutual rights in the General Conference of the Methodist Episcopal Church; now retiring to a life of silence more eloquent than any gift of tongues, having declared his purpose never again to have part in the deliberations of a conference which did not represent the people; now coming forth from his noble retreat to join with his fellow-reformers in the still more noble service of organizing Republican Methodism in America; now carrying the torch of Mutual Rights across the Alleghenies and confirming the faith of thousands and tens of thousands by his untiring ministrations in Cincinnati, in Louisville and in Zanes-

ville, and in all the regions round about; now wielding
in behalf of religious liberty and equality a pen which
was a recognized power in the Christian literature of
his day; now rallying his enfeebled strength in his
seventy-fifth year for a long pilgrimage to the farther
West, journeying on horseback and slow-moving boats
a distance of thousands of miles, passing to and fro between widely-separated conferences, that he might give
a final message and a farewell benediction to his ex-
pectant brethren; and now, last of all, being summoned
to teach young men in preparation for the gospel ministry, hurrying to his glorious task, with his well-
mastered Greek and Latin, his thorough knowledge of
the Book of God as the basis of his theological training,
and, above all, his eloquent Christian manhood, all ready
for instant service at the feet of his Lord, but hearing
in the midst of this last itinerant journey the higher
summons of Heaven, calling him from labor to reward.

And yet Nicholas Snethen, in his unchallenged primacy
among the Fathers, was closely surrounded by a group
of leaders second only to himself. What a glorious company of moral giants God had given to the infant cause
of self-governing Methodism in America! No, the per-
secuted friends of religious liberty were not in want
of brilliant and sacrificial leadership! They had Asa
Shinn, a genius reared in the mountains and untutored
in the schools, and yet so splendidly self-made and God-
made, that he swayed the enraptured thousands of the
proudest city, and, as with the tongue of a Demosthenes,
was armed with a fiery dart for any Macedonian Philip
that dared to threaten the Democracy of the Church;
Asa Shinn, first president of the Ohio Conference, first
president of the Pittsburgh Conference, and, most im-

portant of all, the unanswerable champion of those who, for their simple devotion to the cause of religious liberty, had been cast out of the synagogue of American Methodism.

They had George Brown, the rugged hero of an hundred battles in behalf of the people, a true evangelist in his every pastoral charge, so trenchant and loyal with his pen that he was made editor of the "Western Methodist Protestant," so clear and discriminating in his recollections of itinerant life that he made of them a charming and helpful book for future generations, so faithful through the last lap of the journey of life that, in his seventy-seventh year, he traveled seven thousand miles to meet his waiting audiences.

They had Cornelius Springer, the literary pioneer of the Methodist Protestant Church in the North and the West, who gave alike his talents and his worldly goods, without reservation, to the founding of the paper which was destined to be the forerunner of the "Methodist Recorder." They had Samuel K. Jennings, editor-in-chief of the "Mutual Rights," that valiant periodical which was for so many embattled years the literary fortress of Liberal Methodism, and which was the forerunner of the Methodist Protestant"; Samuel K. Jennings, so versatile and yet so thorough in his mental equipment that, as a preacher, he won the most enthusiastic recognition of his brethren, as a writer, gained distinction at once in the field of religious journalism and in the province of medical science, as a teacher, attained the most notable success, becoming the President of Asbury College in the city of Baltimore; and, as a true believer, fought a good fight and kept the Faith. They had Alexander McCaine, the giant champion of every good cause; the author of that literary thunderbolt entitled "The History and the Mystery of Methodist Episcopacy," a work which, despite all the hysterical outcries raised against it, remained an unanswered challenge to those who had forced upon American Methodism the titles and the tyrannies of an ecclesiastical monarchy. They had John S. Reese, the first of several distinguished leaders of the same family name in the annals of the Maryland Conference and of the denomination; John S. Reese, renowned for his burning eloquence in the pulpit, and so gifted in talent and in disposition for legislative functions that he was many times elected president of the Maryland Conference. They had Dennis B. Dorsey, one of the first victims of Episcopal displeasure, but who, in the hour of his supreme trial, not only braved persecution with noble tranquillity, but, by the very meekness of his unfaltering courage, kindled a torch of sympathy and of kindred heroism in a thousand wavering hearts. They had the good and great William S. Stockton; and, not to speak of others, they had one even greater than he, the Apollos of the American pulpit, Thomas H. Stockton. And, even as Nicholas Snethen stands first as the organizing spirit and the presiding genius among the Fathers of the Methodist Protestant Church, so Thomas H. Stockton stands preëminently first as the pulpit orator among the Fathers; as the inspired voice which made known the mission of liberal Methodism to the American people; a voice which seemed forever saying, as he exclaimed in one of his great messages: "Alas, for all over-government; for all unyielding government; for all idolized government!"

Yes, the Methodist Protestant Church had all these in her early and infant days; and, extending our survey through city and countryside, as history opens to us the story of those heroic days, we might record the names of many other pioneers of our democratic Methodism, every one of whom deserves a book of remembrance. We might recall to the grateful memory of the present generation such noblemen of the Kingdom as Francis Waters, W. H. Wills, Zachariah Ragan, Judge Hopper, Jonathan Flood, Israel Thrapp, W. C. Lipscomb, P. T. Laishley, John Chappell, William Collier, Robert Dobbins, Eli Henkle, Charles Avery, William Hamilton, and, last but not least, that faithful, accurate and comprehensive historian of our Church, Ancel H. Bassett.

The composite example of the Fathers should loom large before us in these days, gathering new force and meaning with every glimpse into that splendid galaxy of shining stars. There were giants in those days; and the Founders of the Methodist Protestant Church deserve enrollment on the brightest pages of the world's religious history.

VII

THE EPOCH OF ORGANIZATION

THE twenty eventful years, from 1828 to 1848, may well be called the period of organization in the Methodist Protestant Church. While the organizing convention was not held until 1830, nor the first General Conference, under constitutional provision, until 1834, yet the Associated Methodist Churches, which were first gathered as independent congregational units around the standard of mutual rights, had been multiplying rapidly ever since the adoption of the Articles of Association, November 12, 1828. From that date onward the number of congregations increased more and more, the spark of liberal Methodism being fanned into flame all the more quickly by the winds of persecution; and, when the cause was finally organized and consolidated by the adoption of a Constitution and Discipline, groups of churches were speedily formed into annual conferences.

This spirit of progress was so much abroad, indeed, and the polity adopted by the founders of our Church was so manifestly in harmony with the genius of America, that within the first twenty years of our history as a denomination some thirty annual conferences had already been organized, beginning with the North Carolina, December 19, 1828, followed at brief intervals by the Maryland, the Ohio, the New York, the Genesee, the Virginia, the Georgia, the West Virginia, the Tennessee, the Alabama, the Onondaga, the South Carolina, the Mississippi, the New Jersey, the Pittsburgh, the

Muskingum, the Indiana, the Michigan, the Illinois, the North Illinois, the Iowa, the South Illinois, the North Indiana, and others still toward the farther northwest and southwest.

In the organic enthusiasm of that aggressive epoch, there was perhaps an over-organization of annual conferences, the fathers having occupied a number of positions which they were unable to consolidate; for they organized a Vermont Conference, a Boston Conference and a Maine Conference, and a few others that later disappeared from the annals of the Church. But such a situation is incidental to every new movement of the Kingdom; and the overflowing enthusiasm which organizes temporarily beyond the bounds of strength to maintain is, in itself, a token of sincerity and of zeal, and, in many circumstances, a token of the inherent strength of the movement; even as the flowing tide, though it ebbs again to the level of the sea, is an evidence to all the world of the throbbing fullness of the great ocean.

And this aggressive spirit, expressing itself in organic enthusiasm, in many instances, even when seemingly fruitless, became the seed-sowing for later harvests. The Texas Conference, for example, was not organized until 1848; but the hand-planting of the Lord which was the sure earnest of that result, occurred even in 1839, when the Tennessee Conference, itself but recently organized, had the courage to establish a mission in the then Republic of Texas, and the missions established by the Ohio Conference became in like manner the seed-corn of the Kingdom which blossomed into conferences as far west as Missouri and Iowa, Kansas and Nebraska, and even on the Pacific Coast.

IX

THE CHURCH OF A THOUSAND BISHOPS

THE Church without a bishop, and yet the Church of a thousand bishops! Such is the paradox that truly expresses the polity of the Methodist Protestant Church in relation to her ministers. It is an elementary principle of our denomination that there is but one order in the ministry; that all elders of the Church of God are equal; and Christian ministers are forbidden to be lords over God's heritage.

But, in accordance with the Biblical meaning of the word bishop, and in harmony with the apostolic interpretation which the word has expressed in apostolic usage, every pastor is a bishop. The word is equivalent to the word shepherd; and the word shepherd is equivalent to the word caretaker. The word bishop signifies an overseer. But whether we call the minister a caretaker or an overseer we presume in either case the same functions. And in either case the original content of the word conveys the idea of leadership, not of overlordship; the idea of protection, but not of tyranny.

The Church of a thousand bishops, because it has so fully realized and exemplified the doctrine of the mutual rights of the ministry and the laity, occupies a unique place in American Methodism. On the one hand this Church is a connectional body, through the appointing power of the annual conference; and on the other hand it is essentially congregational, because of its recognition of the right of the people of every charge to vote on any question; and especially because, in the effectual working of this twofold polity, every pastor enters upon his field of labor with the consciousness that he goes in response to the call of the people, through their instructed delegate, as well as by appointment of the conference.

It must be remembered, however, that mutual rights are bound up with mutual obligations; and every one of the thousand bishops must recognize the local church as the unit of life and as the ultimate source of authority.

The organic unit of our denomination is the individual church. Our fathers fixed and recorded for us a true definition of a church when they wrote into our constitution these words: "A church is a society of believers in Jesus Christ, assembled in any one place for religious worship." In that same place and in that same unit must be found the organic energy of which we are speaking. Those who worship together are peculiarly qualified to work together; and every current of organic energy necessary for the movements of the Kingdom must course through the hearts of those who, like the apostles at Jerusalem, are "all with one accord in one place." And herein also we find the real meaning of organic life in the Kingdom of God. True organization in the Christian Church is not a mechanism, not a machine, not an aggregate of artificial devices. Organic life is associated in the Christian Church with living and believing hearts. The Master said: "I am the vine, ye are the branches." The Apostle Paul, echoing the words of the Saviour, exclaimed: "For as we have many members in the one body, and all members have not the same office, so we, being many, are one body in Christ, and every one members one of another." In such Scriptural sources as these we find the springs of organic energy for every Christian enterprise. Organic life for the Christian Church finds its roots in Christ himself, even as the tree has its roots in the bosom of the earth; every believer is a part of the body of Christ, even as every member is a vital part of the human body.

But while the individual church is the unit of life and organization, the pastor becomes, because of his ordained leadership, the unit of action and of progress. And this remains true, even if every member of the Church is ready and anxious for progressive action; even if, in some instances, the membership appears more responsive to the onward movements of the Kingdom than the pastor himself; simply because the pastor is the ecclesiastical signal officer; because he is at once the bugler that calls to battle and the captain who has been chosen to lead the van.

The future of Democratic Methodism depends very largely upon the various factors of influence which enter into the every-day problems of the local church. These forces must be marshaled and directed to the most efficient ends; and, by common consent, all eyes turn to the pastor as the primary unit of action. There is of course, in every mind, the natural presumption that the pastor possesses the elements of leadership; that he has the talent and the training; that he embodies the spirit of loyalty to every denominational interest; that he can bring to the problems of the Church at once the up-to-date methods of the business world and the devout and prayerful heart which leans last of all upon the grace of God. But, even though the pastor, in certain instances, may lack certain of these qualities of leadership in the progressive development of the Church, does anybody else assume the functions tacitly resigned by the pastor? Not so! By his very office and order, he becomes the specific and exclusive leader in every line of service which the people, by the habit of the centuries, have given over to him. In these highways of activity, therefore, there is no onward movement, unless the pastor leads in the movement. Even though it might occasionally happen that somebody else in the congregation could preach a better sermon than the pastor, nevertheless the pulpit is left entirely to him; and, likewise, in every other distinctively pastoral function, even though there might be some native genius in the congregation who could perform, the one this function and the other that function, and in every case better than the minister himself, yet all these remain, untouched by any human hand, in the separate and exclusive province of the minister.

How great becomes, therefore, the responsibility of the pastor as a unit of action and progress! How dependent are all the allied forces of the Kingdom upon his movements! How great the possible results, if the pastor is wide-awake, alert and progressive!

If the pastor is to make the very most of his influence as the primary unit of progress, he must, first of all, give evidence of his unquestioning faith in his own church. The pastor must believe in his own denomination, and in all her institutions. He must believe in himself and in his mission. No workman in all the world of achievement can succeed, unless he is a genuine optimist as to his own work. If a merchant is a pessimist as to his own goods, who will buy his goods? If an author is a pessimist as to his own ideas, who will adopt his ideas?

If a preacher is a pessimist as to his own message, who will hearken to his message? If the chosen representatives of any given church are pessimists as to that church and its mission, who will join that church in response to their appeal, or support the interests of that church at their solicitation?

Suppose for example that you are selling books, canvassing up and down the country, from house to house. And, to admit the most favorable conditions, suppose that you have one of the best sellers in all the literary world, and that you are canvassing in one of the most intelligent neighborhoods in all America. Nevertheless, if you should come to a man who is a stranger to the book you are trying to sell, and you should spend even five minutes in explaining and elaborating the faults of that book, and close by advising him not to buy it, you could not afterward sell that book to the same man even though you should sing its praises for a thousand years!

And yet there are really those who imagine that they can put a crown of thorns and of mockery upon the brow of their own church, and yet, by a mere flourish of conventional loyalty, persuade others to crown that same church with honor and glory. No ecclesiastical alchemist in all the world can accomplish such a feat as that! Magnify your own church! Honor your own heritage! Believe in your own mission! Be true to your own covenant!

The Church of a thousand bishops realizes also a genuine apostolic succession; a succession of ordained shepherds, each of whom is set apart to the care of the one charge; to the care of one of the gathered flocks of God.

It is beautiful indeed, and equally helpful, to have

faithful and efficient co-laborers, whether they are assistant pastors, unstationed ministers, supernumeraries, superannuates, local preachers or lay-preachers. But the Methodist Protestant Church possesses, as an ideal and as a possibility, two pastors for every charge. And the congregation can have them both for the one salary! The man who has just gone from the conference to his new charge is one of these two pastors, and the man who has just left that charge is the other pastor; for, at a thousand points of contact, these two men are so thoroughly inter-dependent, so abundantly able to help or to hinder, so interwoven in all the warp and woof of their influence, that almost every charge, at the beginning of a conference year, has of necessity two pastors. And there is a profound and hallowed sense in which this relationship might obtain, with reciprocal joy and helpfulness, throughout all the years of every ministry, and to every parish of every denomination in all the Christian world. An unbroken line of Christian pastors, each in turn prophesying good concerning the man who is about to come after him, and each in turn forever speaking well of the man who has just gone before him—that is the true apostolic succession, that is team-work almost divine!

The first step in the formation of this holy alliance is the honest acceptance of it as a simple axiom in pastoral theology. Of course these two men are working together, hand in hand, heart to heart! There should be a consciousness of this relation in every heart in all the Church, including, to the highest degree of mutuality, the two ministers on the charge; the one being physically present, and at his post of duty, day and night; the other being spiritually present, and enlisted with his fellow-laborer in every pastoral function, having bequeathed to his successor in that charge his own pastoral possessions, with his every survey of the parish, his every friendship, his every token of sympathy, his every trophy of conquest, with many prayers for the blessing of God upon the man who has been sent to carry forward the Lord's work.

The pastor who has enough grace and common sense to link up his own work with that of his predecessor, in this partnership of the Kingdom of God, happy indeed is such a minister. On either side of the golden mean in this hallowed relationship, there are two extremes, each of which is to be avoided with equal care. On the one hand nobody wishes any pastor to be a mere imitator of his predecessor in the parish. But, on the other hand, the pastor who goes to a new charge should avoid ultra-independence, and should, as far as possible, project the lines of progress already surveyed by his predecessor, and make intelligent and grateful use of all the data left in his possession. There are pastors who imagine they are called upon to turn aside from every path marked out by those who have gone before them, and that they must blaze their own way, even if they get lost in the wilderness; that their pastoral dignity requires them not alone to pull down the finished structure of the man who has just gone, but that they must even throw away all the building material he had gathered together for the honor of the Lord! What a waste of spiritual resources in such a policy! What an exhibition of pastoral folly! The new pastor can take every result of the former pastor's work, and, without sacrificing a single factor of his independence and originality, can make use of the finished work to the glory of God, to the furtherance of his own plans and to the strengthening of his own initiative.

Inasmuch as the Methodist Protestant Church is the historic champion of the mutual rights of the ministry and the laity, it follows that obligations also are mutual. And every progressive layman in our whole denomination will cheerfully admit that genuine mutuality implies an adequate salary for every pastor.

In approaching this question, however, let us lift the argument at once to the higher plane of service.

The problems of the Kingdom, in this "grand and awful time," are such as to demand the undistracted attention of every minister of the gospel. Therefore, even as a matter of simple economy, the pastor should be relieved of every anxiety which is calculated to weaken or overburden his consecrated powers. An adequate salary, promptly paid at stated intervals, will so increase the value of a pastor, even as a commercial asset, that a people could not make a surer investment, in all the circles of enterprise, than just to raise their pastor's salary! And if it were possible to reckon the worth of the pastor as a moral and spiritual asset in the community, or follow the manifold currents of influence which are released in his life, when worldly cares are removed, what people would then refuse their minister the few additional shekles which would afford him the sinews of manly independence? If your pastor really needs an increase of fifty per cent in his salary, and if the community really knows that he needs it, then you can raise the larger salary next year with a good deal less labor and worry than you have hitherto expended in raising the smaller salary! Why is it so? Because the pride of a community in its own church, and in its own resident minister, has a distinct market value, and you can cash it at any moment, by simply showing that the cause you represent has a face value equivalent to the sum you ask for! Methodist Protestants are among the richest Christians in America, in the recognized value of their polity and of their heritage; but they have sometimes been very slow in collecting their rightful dividends, and in cashing their honorable coupons!

The Church of a thousand bishops, in view of our ever-widening opportunity, needs another thousand bishops!

Every Christian Church in America, every sect of Christians in all the earth, is calling men to enter the Lord's harvest field; and every voice of persuasion is echoing the ancient cry: "Lift up your eyes and look on the fields; for they are white already to harvest!" "The harvest truly is great, but the laborers are few: pray ye therefore the Lord of the harvest, that he will send forth laborers into the harvest."

The proportion of young men entering the gospel ministry is very much less, by every classification, than it was in the days of our fathers, and less than even a few short years ago. The college students of to-day are giving themselves, in ever-increasing proportions, to the secular professions; to the law, to medicine, to literature; or else to the inviting opportunities of commercial life. And the influence of the great war has doubtless quickened the secular trend of the youth of every land, for a little while; though we believe the ultimate result of the great conflict will be favorable to the Church and to the Kingdom of God. But the responsibility of this situation rests largely with the churches. The claims of the ministry upon the talent of the Christian have not been clearly and heartily recognized.

And herein lies the first hope of new recruits for the ranks of the ministry. The young Christian himself must learn to harken to the voice of God. The young Samuel answered, "Here am I!" The young Christian of to-day is prone to disregard the heavenly voices and heavenly visions, or to interpret them as meant for somebody else. But the command of the Christ, "Go ye out into all the world and preach the gospel," is an injunction not alone to the apostles already enlisted in the ranks of the ministry. These words of the Master constitute a general invitation to the disciples and believers of the whole world; and every young Christian should realize that he has no right to turn away from this divine claim upon his life until, by a most thorough self-examination, and by a prayer of self-surrender to the will of God, he has discovered his divinely-appointed work in the world. And he should enter upon this high test with a willing-heartedness which will evidence his sincerity.

If he is thus made to feel that he is not qualified for the ministry, or that his aptitudes and predilections are so strongly inclined to some other calling as to make the ministry impossible to his conscience, then indeed is he released from the universal call to the Christian Church. But every man who is born into the Kingdom of Heaven; every man who enjoys the witnessing presence of the Holy Spirit; every man who has really and truly become a disciple of the Lord Jesus, should put to himself, in prayerful sincerity, this question: "Am I called to the gospel ministry?" And, in seeking an answer to this question, he has no right to claim supernatural tokens or

indications of his call. The dispensation of the Holy
Spirit is a dispensation of duty, as revealed to men
through the spiritual needs that lie before them, and
through the still small voice of a conscience enlightened
of God. "Here is the ripened harvest; here am I with
a sickle in my strong right hand; what answer can I
give to God, if I fail to reap and gather in?" That is
the true logic of Christian duty, and the self-challenge
that should answer to the call of God in the heart of
every Christian who is qualified to become a co-worker
with the great Shepherd and Bishop of souls.

X

WOMAN'S RIGHTS IN THE MODERN PULPIT

THE Methodist Protestant Church was founded chiefly on the principle of the mutual rights of ministers and laymen; but our denomination, at a later period, enjoyed the happy and cherished privilege of taking the initiative also in the recognition of the mutual rights of men and women. While the Mother Church of American Methodism was still unwilling to venture the ordination even of the most gifted Christian women to the Gospel Ministry, the Methodist Protestant Church welcomed a number of elect ladies of manifest ability and consecration to her pulpits, and to every function of an ordained ministry.

At the very first step of this new departure of Democratic Methodism in America, Anna Howard Shaw came to us from her parish in Massachusetts, bearing in her hands the most abundant evidence of her educational equipment for the work to which she had dedicated herself. And both because she was the first fruits of our recognition of the mutual rights of men and women in the Kingdom of God, and because of the well-deserved fame of this truly great woman, her name will stand, through the generations, at the head of the pioneer list of the ordained women of the Churches of Christ in America. Anna Howard Shaw served her generation with the moral enthusiasm of a martyr; and while the times were ultimately favorable to the cause she espoused, and while other great leaders shared the glory of her final victory, yet she would have fought the battle alone against all the world, on her own initiative; and if the cause had demanded the supreme sacrifice, she would have gone with jubilant feet to a martyr's death.

Born at New-Castle-on-Tyne, and coming to America with her parents in early childhood, Anna Howard Shaw was a full-rounded Anglo-Saxon, uniting in herself the genuine spirit of both hemispheres; possessing at once the dogged persistence of the Briton and the unfailing optimism of the true American. Her sense of humor, the saving quality of every fighter in a good cause, became in the career of this noble reformer still another kind of genius; and she laughed off many a burden which would have broken other hearts. This gift divine always came to the aid of her patience, her tolerance and her generosity, in every crisis of her embattled life, and even as it aided her in winning the victory, it surely sweetened her triumph at the last, and added not a little to the sunset glory of her great life.

The crowning gift of Dr. Shaw, the one talent which was clearly reflected in all others, was her straightforward common sense. But hers was a common sense endowed with vision, and with a boundless hope for humanity. Her logical grip on the great questions of the age, as well as her rugged readiness at any moment for the hardest kind of a battle in a worthy cause, gave a masculine tinge to her genius. And yet she was the soul of gentleness; and all womanly graces were angel-big in her every thought and action.

In the Beekman Avenue Methodist Protestant Church, at Tarrytown-on-the-Hudson, October 12, 1880, Anna Howard Shaw was ordained to the gospel ministry.

Dr. Shaw in her autobiography has given the author of this book, then pastor of the Tarrytown Church, all too much credit for her final victory in the long struggle for recognition.   It is indeed true that he opened wide the doors of the local church; and, with the eager help of the progressive laymen of the congregation, secured the necessary recommendations; and he also had the pleasure of bringing forward the argument of the hour.   But in all this the pastor was simply a co-worker with other progressives; with such men as Rev. Dr. Mark Staple and Rev. Dr. Charles Edgar Wilbur, both of whom, together with Mr. Theodore Cocheu, and other leaders of the ministry and the laity, contributed in a most essential way to the final result. It may be of interest to our readers to know that on this occasion there was no extended debate on the abstract question of the ordination of women. In our support of Anna Howard Shaw we emphasized, not the universal rule of the Church up to that hour, and not our desire to reverse these precedents of the ages, but rather we emphasized the notable exception which we truly believed it right to make. Our argument was something like this: if a candidate for the ministry appears before this conference, and gives evidence of having "all the gifts, graces and acquirements" essential to the office of an elder; if this candidate possesses natural talents for the ministry which, taken together, constitute a perfect genius for the ministry; and if, as a training for these natural powers, the candidate has received the most thorough education, at once in the field of science and in the field of theology; and if there is superadded to these gifts and acquirements a self-consecration which is so vital and sincere as to become a living sacrifice—

given such a candidate, shall the ordination be refused simply because this candidate is a woman? We encamped around this one argument and sought no other; and the ordination followed on the day after the decisive vote was taken. We clearly foresaw that our candidate would fully justify what we did that day at Tarrytown-on-the-Hudson. Anna Howard Shaw not only justified the day of her ordination, but she even glorified it. Her whole life, from her earliest childhood in the woods of Michigan to the end of her great career, was one long battle for the right. She finally resigned her pastoral office to devote herself entirely to the achievement of the equal rights of women; and her last triumphal years, though accompanied with many personal afflictions, must have been very comforting to her ardent soul, as she approached, by swift stages, the final goal of the Olympic race. And so great and elemental was her sense of justice that, if she had lived in some land of the Amazons, where women alone held the scepter or the ballot, Anna Howard Shaw would have fought there for the rights of men.

Rev. Dr. Lee Anna Starr, an ordained minister of the North Illinois Conference, occupies a place among the elect ladies of our Church second only to that of Dr. Anna Howard Shaw. Dr. Starr has served with great efficiency in the pastoral office, as well as having made a distinguished name for herself on the lecture platform under the auspices of the Woman's Christian Temperance Union. Her pastoral career includes a period of service with the college church at Adrian, Michigan, with the Avalon Park Church, Chicago, and with the South Park Church, Canton, Illinois.

As a public lecturer Dr. Starr has appeared on the

platform in almost every state in the union, and her message has carried conviction on the temperance question to tens of thousands of delighted hearers.

Dr. Starr is now writing a book on the Biblical status of women; and her thorough acquaintance with the Hebrew language, as well as with the literature of her subject from first to last, admirably fits her for this timely service to the Church and to the world. In this work the Edenic position of woman is to be surveyed, this province of thought to include both the period before the Fall and after the Fall. She will devote three chapters to the study of Genesis 3:16, wherein appears the divine Word, "Thy desire shall be to thy husband."

Later she will discuss the antediluvian status of woman, and later still her social and religious state under the Mosaic dispensation. Coming finally to the New Testament dispensation, she will include in her survey (1) the teachings of Christ on the subject, (2) the teachings and implications of the Book of the Acts of the Apostles, and finally the Pauline teaching.

Prominent among the ordained women of the Methodist Protestant Church is Rev. Eugenia St. John, of the Kansas Conference. She was ordained in 1889 at Haddam, Kansas, and has served seven churches in a most acceptable manner and left them in good condition. Gordon Place Church, Kansas City, and the London Heights Church, Kansas City, are included in these charges, as well as Neosho Rapids, Emporia, Harland and Bellaire. Mrs. St. John has been busy on the lecture platform, as well as in the pulpit; and her success as a pastor and as a public speaker, as well as her courageous championship of the rights of women in the Christian Church, has made her one of the leading figures in the progressive movement which opened wide the official doors of our denomination to our gifted women. Mrs. St. John was a brave and efficient leader in the battle for prohibition, and during the Great War she spent a year at Fort Riley, ministering to the overseas wounded, under appointment of the Women's Christian Temperance Union.

Other talented women ordained by the Kansas Conference are Gertrude Campbell, a graduate of Aurora College, Illinois, ordained in 1893; Miss Rosa Watson, also a college graduate, ordained in 1889; Rev. Matilda McBride, ordained in 1893; Miss Rosetta Smith, ordained in 1889. Miss Smith served six pastorates faithfully and founded a church at Ash Grove, which is still prosperous.

In addition to the ordained women already recorded in these pages, there are a number of faithful ministers of the gospel distributed among the conferences, whose names deserve to be mentioned as belonging to the advance guard in the army of chosen handmaidens of the Lord, who will doubtless soon fill many of the needy fields of the Kingdom of Christ. Among these are Mrs. J. R. Waggoner, Mrs. D. P. York, of the Onondaga Conference; Rev. Ada Luke, and Rev. Mrs. Gray of the Michigan Conference; Rev. Bertha Larson, of the North Illinois Conference. Miss Larson, who is a young woman of keenest intellect and of the most unselfish devotion to the Lord's work, is now in the McCormick Theological Seminary, Chicago.

Rev. Hallie A. Beck, of the Onondaga, and Rev. Mary E. Bartlett, of the Louisiana, are performing active and efficient service in their respective conferences.

XI

OUR PERIODICAL LITERATURE

I. THE "METHODIST PROTESTANT"

THE "Methodist Protestant" is not only the senior periodical of the Methodist Protestant Church, but the oldest weekly periodical in American Methodism, having continued in unbroken royal line from the "Wesleyan Repository," which began its career April 12, 1821. William S. Stockton, a progressive and influential layman of the Methodist Episcopal Church, living within the bounds of the Philadelphia Conference was the editor of the "Wesleyan Repository"; and with such ability and courage did he pursue this worthy enterprise that he is recognized as one of the founders of the Methodist Protestant Church. This periodical which was published in magazine form was first printed in Trenton, New Jersey, and afterward in Philadelphia, and continued for three years giving way to the "Mutual Rights."

The "Repository" was not devoted entirely to the cause of lay-representation, but began with the announcement that the magazine would welcome "essays relating to Church Government, discipline or usages, under the proper restrictions of truth, charity, peace and brotherly kindness, as enjoined in the gospel." The "Mutual Rights," which ran its great career from August, 1824, to July, 1828, was edited by Dr. Samuel K. Jennings, who was supported by a committee acting with the functions of a directory; and this periodical became in all respects the oracle of Democratic Methodism as opposed to the growing autocracy of the Mother Church. In September, 1828, the name of this tribune of the people was slightly changed, and it appeared as the "Mutual Rights and Christian Intelligencer"; Rev. Dennis B. Dorsey being the editor.

The "Methodist Protestant" began its splendid career January 7, 1831, and although for a few years at a later period the additional name of "Family Visitor" was linked with the name now so well known to the world, it is historically true to say that the "Methodist Protestant" traces its pedigree to April 12, 1821, the birthday of the freedom of the press in American Methodism, and its own distinguished history to January 7, 1831. Among the famous editors of the earlier history of the "Methodist Protestant" were Rev. E. Yates Reese, Rev. Nicholas Snethen, Rev. Asa Shinn, Rev. Augustus Webster, Rev. J. T. Murray, and Rev. E. J. Drinkhouse.

During an eventful period, including the stormy days of the Civil War, the editorial management of the "Methodist Protestant" was put in commission, being conducted by distinguished ministers of the Maryland Conference, who performed the editorial functions in connection with arduous pastoral duties. These commissions included men of splendid editorial ability, and a number of them, sooner or later, served brief periods, each in turn, as the sole editor of the paper; and so faithfully did these men perform their editorial duties that the epoch covered by their contributions shines forth among the brightest epochs in the evolution of our periodical literature. A number of the most famous editors of the "Methodist Protestant" served long periods with unusual distinction in that capacity. Rev. E. Yates Reese, D.D., occupied the sanctum for twenty years; Rev. Augustus Webster, D.D., three years; Rev. J. T. Murray, D.D., four years; Rev. E. J. Drinkhouse, D.D., eighteen years, and Rev. Francis T. Tagg, D.D., twenty-four years.

Dr. Drinkhouse who gave eighteen years in distinguished service to the Church through the editorial pages of the "Methodist Protestant," and who is the author of the well-known "History of Methodist Reform," established the claim of the "Methodist Protestant" as the oldest Methodist paper in the United States.

Through twenty-four eventful years Rev. Dr. Francis T. Tagg was the editor of the "Methodist Protestant," and his editorial genius added very greatly to the influence and fame of this oldest of our church periodicals. He had already fulfilled a noble career before entering upon his editorial mission. He was for several years secretary of the Board of Missions of the Methodist Protestant Church, and did much of the heroic and progressive work which established this great cause in the hearts of our people. In 1888 he went to London as our denominational representative in the World's Missionary Congress, and again served in that capacity in 1905 when the Congress was held in New York City. He has served twice as a member of the Ecumenical Conference of Methodism; once at its meeting in London in 1901, and again at its meeting in Toronto, Canada, in 1911. He was president of the General Conference from 1904 to 1908; and prior to these larger denominational honors, he served a number of leading churches in the Maryland Conference, his work from first to last being fruitful of great results for the Kingdom. A strong, clear-cut, trenchant and fearless writer, his pen a bold and aggressive champion of every moral reform, Dr. Tagg's noble and eventful life has been one of the great determining influences of the Methodist Protestant Church.

Since the voluntary retirement of Dr. Tagg in 1916, Rev. Dr. Frank T. Benson has been editor of the "Methodist Protestant." He was elected by the unanimous vote of the General Conference at Zanesville, Ohio, and entered at once upon his editorial mission. A successful career in the pastoral office, during which he served prominent churches of Baltimore and Washington, prepared him for sympathetic approach to the people; and his message, whether it takes the form of a sermon or an editorial, is always to the point. The refined simplicity of his literary style has won him the heart of the Church; and he is so loyal to the larger program of the denomination, so wide awake to every good cause, so alert to the spirit of this new day, and yet so true to the worthy traditions of the past, that everybody is made to realize that Dr. Benson is, beyond question, the right man in the right place.

The Baltimore Directory of the Board of Publication of the Methodist Protestant Church is comprised of the following ministers and laymen:—Rev. George W. Haddaway, D.D., Rev. Roby F. Day, D.D., Mr. H. A. Abbott, Mr. George Mather and Mr. Edwin Cover. The thriving business of the Baltimore headquarters has long been established at 316 North Charles Street. But a printing plant has recently been secured, with facilities adequate not only to the production of the Methodist Protestant itself, but to the demands of the growing vol-

ume of outside work. Among the former publishing
agents of the Baltimore house were Mr. William J. C.
Dulany and Rev. Thomas R. Woodford, both of whom
rendered faithful and distinguished service to the church.
The present agent, Mr. Charles Reiner, Jr., is an ener-
getic and progressive man, and is giving a good account
of his important stewardship.

II. THE "METHODIST RECORDER"

The "Methodist Recorder" was officially created by
action of the General Conference of 1854, that body
authorizing the publication of a new paper to be called
the "Western Methodist Protestant," and providing at
the same time for a Western book concern. But the
"Methodist Recorder" had an important forerunner, of
a semi-official kind, in a paper known as the "Western
Recorder"; and even this latter periodical had its transitory contemporaries in such papers as the "Methodist
Correspondent" and the "Methodist Protestant Letter-
Press," all these literary ventures being an outgrowth of
the spirit of the North and the West, which sought freedom of expression on the great public questions then
agitating the Church and the nation.

In response to this popular demand, and under the
initial auspices of the Pittsburgh Conference, supported
immediately by the Ohio Conference, and in rapid succession by other conferences, Rev. Cornelius Springer
established, in the year 1839, near Zanesville, Ohio,
the "Western Recorder"; and under the sturdy genius
of Mr. Springer and his collaborators, this publication
attained a far-reaching influence. In 1845, with the approval of the entire group of sustaining annual conferences, the "Western Recorder" was purchased by that

scholarly Christian gentleman, Rev. Ancel H. Bassett, who conducted the paper through ten eventful years, and made it still more decisively an oracle of the Church. As a loyal and logical sequence, therefore, the convention of supporting annual conferences which met in Zanesville, November 1, 1854, for the purpose of carrying out the provision of the General Conference, immediately recognized the semi-official status of the "Western Recorder," and, having purchased the paper from its private owners, changed its name to that of the "Western Methodist Protestant," and reëstablished it in Springfield, Ohio. Doctor Bassett was officially elected both editor and publisher of the new paper, and became denominationally the first editor of the "Methodist Recorder" under its earlier official name as the "Western Methodist Protestant." But the "Western Recorder" was recognized as so essentially the oracle of the North and the West, through the sixteen epoch-making years of its history, and its semi-official character as representing a group of supporting conferences, and as being so genuine a tribune of the people, that the name of Cornelius Springer will forever stand as that of the first editor of the "Methodist Recorder."

Doctor Bassett continued to serve in the double capacity of editor and publisher until 1860, when Dr. George Brown was elected editor, Doctor Bassett continuing as publisher. After two years of ardent service in the editorial chair, Doctor Brown retired, and was succeeded by Rev. Dennis B. Dorsey, Jr. In 1864, both Dorsey and Bassett resigned, and John Scott was elected editor, with Rev. Joel S. Thrapp as publishing agent. At the next General Conference, in 1866, Doctor Thrapp retired from the publishing agency, being succeeded by

Ancel H. Bassett; but Doctor Scott remained in office until 1870, when that brilliant writer, Alexander Clark, became editor of the "Methodist Recorder" and gave himself a living sacrifice to the work until his lamented death, which occurred July 6, 1879.

The official act of union with the Wesleyan Methodists carried with it a change of name for our Church; and from that time until the re-union with the South, in 1877, our denomination was known as the Methodist Church, and the name of the "Western Methodist Protestant" was accordingly changed to that of the "Methodist Recorder." In 1871, the publishing house and the paper were removed from Springfield, Ohio, to Pittsburgh, Pennsylvania. Soon after the death of Alexander Clark, Dr. John Scott was called to his second term of service as editor of the "Methodist Recorder," and he remained at his post of duty, an efficient servant of the Church, until 1888, when he was succeeded by President D. S. Stephens, of Adrian College, who gave eight years of the most fruitful period of his splendid life to the editorial conduct of this journal, and then retired to become chancellor of the Kansas City University. Dr. Martin Luther Jennings, successor to Dr. Stephens, was editor of the "Recorder" for twelve years, and left the stamp of his own nobility and of his indelible influence alike upon the character of the paper and upon the minds of his readers.

Since the lamented death of Dr. Jennings in 1913, the author of this book has been editor of the "Methodist Recorder."

There is one episode in the evolution of the "Methodist Recorder" which deserves a permanent record in the story of our periodical literature. We ask our readers to go back for a moment to the meeting of the General Conference of our denomination in the city of Pittsburgh, in the month of May, 1838. There was a heated controversy in that session on the slavery question; for the shadow of that great problem was then over the whole land. And while no final deliverance was made against the institution of slavery on behalf of the denomination at that time, the question being tacitly left to the sentiment and judgment of the annual conferences, yet the principle involved was too fundamental and world-wide, and had become too aggressive to be surrendered even to the spirit of compromise. When therefore the conference was discussing the report of the committee on the conduct and policy of the Church paper, the slavery controversy again reappeared in the form of a resolution requiring that all matter on the subject of slavery should be excluded from the columns of the official organ. At this juncture, Dr. George Brown, finally gaining the recognition of the president and the ear of the assembly, called attention to the fact that no such limitation could be put upon the editor of a church paper, the constitution of the Methodist Protestant Church expressly declaring that "no rule shall be passed infringing the liberty of speech or of the press." The re-discovery of the glorious corner-stone of liberty upon which the Methodist Protestant Church forever rests, together with the increasing momentum of Christian sentiment in America against the sin of slavery, hushed at once the debate of the General Conference, while the authoritative nature of the evidence in the case calmed the spirit of controversy and restored the mutual good will of all who had taken part in the parliamentary battle.

But there was an important sequel to the whole discussion, and one which came too late for the immediate cognizance of the General Conference. The great Thomas H. Stockton was elected editor of the Church paper; and in due time the editor-elect repaired to Baltimore to assume the duties of his office. But the Baltimore Book Committee, ignoring the action of the General Conference, and in direct violation of the Constitution of the Church, and, even of still greater importance, in crucifixion of the very spirit of liberty to which our Church was dedicated from the beginning, forbade the publishing of any literary matter on the question of slavery. To his own perpetual honor, and to the glory of the Church of mutual-rights and of human freedom, the famous Stockton instantly resigned, leaving the editorial office to anybody who might be willing to carry out what he truly called "the violent undoing of the arrangement made by the General Conference."

But the deeper meaning of the epoch-making hours at Pittsburgh in 1838 is to be found in the elemental principle of liberty written by the fathers into the original Constitution of the Methodist Protestant Church: "No rule shall be passed infringing the liberty of speech or of the press!" The primal element of freedom, refluent in the very life-blood of the founders of our beloved Church, and engraved forever in our fundamental law, has arrayed our people in every epoch with the progressive forces of the Christian world. That constitutional provision, committing our Church to freedom of speech, through tongue and pen, for all generations, becomes a golden link binding us with all the ancient prophets of human liberty, from Lincoln and Washington across the ages to Calvary, and to him who is the perennial source of all true liberty in Church and State.

Turning to the financial management of the "Methodist Recorder" and of the Sunday-school papers at Pittsburgh, we find a record of faithful and efficient service on the part of our successive publishing agents. Dr. Ancel H. Bassett was succeeded in the business management by Rev. James Robison, who served the cause with loving fidelity for many years. He was in turn succeeded by William McCracken, who was a progressive and loyal servant of the Church, and who devoted himself without reserve to the upbuilding of our periodical literature. Professor W. S. Fleming of West Virginia gave a good account of his stewardship in this important office and sustained the best traditions of that well-known family in the business management of the paper. Mr. F. W. Pierpont was publishing agent of the "Methodist Recorder" through a long and eventful period of time, 1896 to 1920, and his far-seeing business methods in the management of the office deserved the high tribute which was paid to his work by his repeated reëlection to this responsible position. The General Conference of 1920 elected Mr. L. H. Neiplin publishing agent for our Pittsburgh headquarters, and he has entered upon the work by the introduction of up-to-date methods in every department of the business. The members of the Pittsburgh Directory are as follows: Rev. Dr. C. E. Sheppard, Rev. Dr. C. M. Lippincott, Mr. A. M. Lyons, Mr. Robert Rawsthorne, Jr., and Mr. Felix Blaising.

The Pittsburgh property belonging to the Board of Publication of the Methodist Protestant Church has an approximate value of $300,000. A permanent headquarters, apart from the above-named property, has recently been acquired at 613 West Diamond, N. S., Pittsburgh; and this building is at once so ample and so well adapted to the work as to constitute a genuine home for the "Methodist Recorder," the Sunday-School papers and the book business.

SUNDAY-SCHOOL PERIODICALS

The Sunday-school literature of the Methodist Protestant Church began as an humble adjunct to the regular Church periodicals, the "Methodist Protestant" and the "Methodist Recorder"; but the progressive development of our Sunday-school papers has been one of the notable products of our denominational life. At the earlier period the quarterlies were produced at Baltimore, under the direction of the editor of the "Methodist Protestant," while the papers, "Our Morning Guide" and "Our Children," were published at Pittsburgh, under the direction of the editor of the "Methodist Recorder." The people of the passing generations perhaps never realized our denominational debt of grateful recognition to the busy editors of the "Protestant" and the "Recorder" for their zealous and self-sacrificing devotion to the Church through their splendid work on the Sunday-school papers.

In 1884 the Sunday-school periodicals, as a whole, were made a separate literary department, and were transferred to Pittsburgh, Rev. John F. Cowan, D.D., becoming editor of the entire group of papers and lesson helps. Dr. Cowan, whose thirteen years in the work has left a permanent literary impression upon our Sunday-schools, resigned in 1897 to become associate editor of the "Christian Endeavor World." During a brief interregnum, Anna Pierpont Siviter was acting editor, and this well-known writer produced during that period some of her best fugitive pieces in prose and poetry.

September 1, 1898, marks the beginning of a new and important era in the evolution of our Sunday-school literature; for on that date Rev. Charles Edgar Wilbur, D.D., L.L.D., was elected editor of the whole series of periodicals; and the twenty-two years since that date have witnessed phenomenal growth, at once in the number of papers and helps sent forth to the Church, in the aggregate circulation of the whole body of our Sunday-school literature, and in the unsurpassed average of literary quality which characterizes the series. Ten Sunday-school periodicals are produced under his editorial direction, and the aggregate circulation of this literature is two hundred and five thousand copies with every issue. Dr. Wilbur is a clear and forceful writer and an indefatigable worker, while his facile and experienced pen is fortified by accurate knowledge in the field of Biblical literature, and by a literary judgment which quickly grasps the heart of his every theme. During the past year the Board of Publication was asked to loan Dr. Wilbur to the Administrative Committee for Relief in the Near East, and as a member of this Sunday-school Commission, he visited Armenia and other parts of the Turkish Empire, joining heartily and efficiently in an important survey of material and religious conditions in all that region.

This latest experience, together with his journey around the world as a member of the Commission of the World's Sunday-school Association, under the auspices of Mr. H. J. Heinz, and also a brief period of observation and study in the Holy Land, has still further equipped Dr. Wilbur for his great work. Our Sunday-school periodicals under his editorial hand are unsurpassed in America, and a number of the ten periodicals have a wide circulation in the Sunday-schools of other denominations.

THE "METHODIST PROTESTANT HERALD"

In the development of the periodical literature of the Methodist Protestant Church, many religious papers of a semi-official kind were started by different annual conferences, and others still through individual enterprise. Our official organs, indeed, are largely the final outgrowth of these unofficial and semi-official forerunners; for the "Methodist Protestant Letter Press," and the "Western Recorder" represented the first two steps toward the "Methodist Recorder," while the "Mutual Rights" was a link in the chain that led to the "Methodist Protestant."

One of the most successful of these annual conference papers, and one which has been continuously prosperous for many years, is the "Methodist Protestant Herald," edited and published by Rev. Dr. J. F. McCulloch, at Greensboro, North Carolina. The evolution of this semi-official paper is very interesting. About the beginning of the Civil War, Rev. J. L. Michaux published for our people in North Carolina a weekly paper called "The Watchman and Harbinger"; and from 1874 to 1890 "The Central Methodist Protestant." The name of Rev. J. L. Michaux is entitled to a place of honor because of his worthy effort to meet a real need of our Church in this important field.

The "Methodist Protestant Herald," at first and for years called "Our Church Record," was started in 1894, and has been continued uninterruptedly to the present.

In a short time it became evident to the publisher that the income of the "Herald" must be supplemented, and he appealed to friends of the paper and of the Church to contribute to the erection of a publishing house in the business center of Greensboro, to provide not only offices for the paper, but also revenue to be derived from rents. About $5,000 was contributed in sums from $500 down, and a building was provided at a cost of about $8,000. The debt thus incurred was paid from the rents of the building. This property has increased in value until now it would sell for $60,000.

Rev. Dr. J. F. McCulloch, editor of the "Methodist Protestant Herald," is a man of many talents, and he has won distinction at once as minister, educator and editor. He was for a term of years a professor in Adrian College, and afterward became president of that institution, fulfilling the important duties of this high office with signal fidelity and ability; and his editorial gifts are manifest to all his readers. He is a steadfast and eloquent apostle of Democratic Methodism in America, and whether on the General Conference floor, or in the columns of his paper, he is true to the legacy of the fathers, and to the cause of freedom and self-government in Church and State.

THE WOMAN'S "MISSIONARY RECORD"

The "Missionary Record," published under the auspices of the Woman's Foreign Missionary Society of the Methodist Protestant Church, had its forerunner in a paper called the "Methodist Missionary," edited and published by Rev. T. H. Colhouer, D.D. Pastoral duties prevented Dr. Colhouer's continuance of the work he had so well begun, and the paper was taken over by Rev.

C. H. Williams, at that time corresponding secretary of the Board of Missions, who re-christened it the "Methodist Protestant Missionary."

A little later, and just when the Woman's Foreign Missionary Society seriously considered the publication of an official organ, the Denominational Board of Missions, on their own prompting, offered to turn over the Methodist Protestant Missionary to the Woman's Foreign Missionary Society. This overture was accepted, and the paper, being adopted, was re-named the "Woman's Missionary Record," Mrs. Mary A. Miller becoming its first editor. The first issue appeared in July, 1885, and carried the following motto suggested by Mrs. W. K. Gillespie: "I can do all things through Christ which strengtheneth me."

The editors of the "Record," with their period of service, have been as follows: Mrs. Mary A. Miller, ten years; Mrs. Mathilda McBride, two years; Mrs. F. C. Huling, four years; Mrs. H. T. Stephens, one year; Mrs. J. F. McCulloch, eighteen years.

The "Missionary Record" was published for ten years and more by Dr. J. F. McCulloch, editor of the "Methodist Protestant Herald." Mrs. E. C. Chandler, author of the interesting and comprehensive little book entitled "History of the Woman's Foreign Missionary Society," testifies that Dr. McCulloch's "watchfulness and economy saved the Society many dollars."

The present editor of the "Missionary Record" is Mrs. H. E. Amos of Cambridge, Ohio, and the "Missionary Record," with an ever-growing circulation and influence, is published from that city.

XII

THE CALL TO FOREIGN FIELDS

THE history of Christian civilization, from the days of the great apostle who harkened to the Macedonian cry, has been simply the history of the outgoing missionary energy of the Christian Church, elaborated on the pages of the nations by the logical forces of the faith. Out among the Greeks, out among the Romans, out among the Britons, out among the Germans, out among the Russians, out among the Indians, out among the blindest pagans, out into darkest Africa, out into the farthest Orient—all the outgoings of the gospel of Jesus Christ have simply described the progress of foreign missions. And civilization itself, with all the social reforms of the ages, has simply waited upon the onward march of the missionaries of the Cross. The one thing needful to-day in every turbulent and distracted country in the world, is not the incoming of any fragmentary elements or separate units of civilization, but the incoming of the great comprehensive principle, the vitalizing and developing force of Christianity as a spiritual reality. This alone is the possible salvation for men and nations. The foreign missionary has always been not only the forerunner of a personal Saviour, but the pioneer of the highest civilization.

The missionary zeal of the Methodist Protestant Church found expression in the first General Conference of the denomination in 1834, when a board of foreign missions was duly organized; and two years later a missionary was sent to Africa. But the denomination was so entirely preoccupied with the work of establishing itself in America that it could not function as yet in foreign lands. And while at later periods, the board elected still other missionaries, it was not until 1880 that the missionary spirit of the Church emerged in actual achievement. Miss Lizzie M. Guthrie left Pittsburgh for Japan April 22, 1880, to become the first foreign missionary under appointment of the Methodist Protestant Church; and, on the lamented death of this faithful pioneer, she was succeeded in the work by Miss Harriet G. Brittain.

But while the educational initiative had been taken, and splendid beginnings had been realized, the Methodist Protestant Church did not come into being in Japan, as an ecclesiastical unit, until July 11, 1886, when Rev. Dr. Fred C. Klein, the first ordained missionary of the denomination in the foreign field, organized a church at Yokohama, and followed this initial enterprise by organizing another church at Nagoya in November, 1887, five months after his arrival in that city. Dr. Klein had previously spent two years and more in Yokohama, where he arrived from America September 23, 1883, and where he had organized and developed a night school, which became afterward the real nursery of the Church in that region. Dr. Klein was also the founder of Nagoya College, which is now the educational joy and pride of our denomination in the Orient. Mrs. Fred C. Klein, always a wise and zealous coworker with her husband in that vast new field of service, organized the first Junior Endeavor Society in Nagoya.

Rev. Dr. T. H. Colhouer, accompanied in the voyage

and in all his subsequent activities by his faithful and gifted companion, reached Japan in May, 1887; and to this distinguished author and minister of our denomination belongs the honor of building the first house of worship under the auspices of the Methodist Protestant Church in a foreign land.

The Japan Conference was organized September 15, 1892, three American ministers and one Japanese constituting the whole conference. The evolution of the Methodist Protestant Mission field in the Orient has been of a constant, healthful and permanent kind; and the Japan Mission Conference now has 18 regularly organized churches, 50 chapel organizations and appointments, 18 ordained native ministers, 13 other preachers and evangelists in the pastoral field, 2,119 communicants, and 3,649 Sunday-school scholars. In the various Methodist Protestant schools of Japan there are more than one thousand enrolled students, 500 of these being in Nagoya College alone.

The Methodist Protestant Church has more recently entered the door of opportunity in the broad missionary fields of India and China, and while the denomination has not as yet entirely consolidated its position in either of those countries, hopeful progress is being made, both in the educational province and in direct evangelism. The work at Kalgan, China, is now being developed under the joint auspices of the Board of Foreign Missions and the Woman's Foreign Missionary Society; and the mission at Dhulia, India, also gives promise of splendid results. The one challenge supreme in the missionary field of the Methodist Protestant Church arises from the distinct responsibility which rests upon the denomination for the spiritual shepherding of tens of thousands of people.

In October, 1919, the Board of Foreign Missions sent a missionary deputation to the Orient to make a practical survey of our whole field of opportunity. For this important service, the Board selected Rev. Dr. Fred C. Klein, for many years the faithful and efficient corresponding secretary of the Board, and also the first ordained missionary of our denomination in foreign lands, and as his companion on the deputation, Rev. Dr. John C. Broomfield, the recording secretary of the Board, and the president of the Forward Movement Commission of the last quadrennium. After a sojourn of several months in our foreign fields, during which time they visited, not only all our mission stations of Japan, of China and of India, but also the outlying fields of possibility in those three great countries, they returned in time to make a report of their findings to the General Conference at Greensboro; a report which gave at once a great new impulse to missionary sentiment among our people, and brought home to the denomination, as never before, a realization of the opportunity and the obligation that awaits the Church in those ripening fields of the Lord's harvest.

These two men were highly qualified to make a comprehensive survey of our whole missionary field in the Far East. Dr. Klein's long and brilliant career in the service of the board, first as an aggressive and fruitful missionary in Japan, and in later years as the untiring champion of foreign missions among the churches, made him an expert in missionary affairs, and will enable him to exercise that decisive and trustworthy judgment which is so important to our work in the Orient at this critical hour. Dr. Broomfield, though zealously engrossed in the pastoral administration of his large and growing church at Fairmont, and though giving much time, with splendid results, in the Million-Dollar campaign and in the war-time service of his country, has found opportunity to inform himself very thoroughly as to the missionary enterprises of the age. Both of these apostles of the "Go ye into all the world" gospel are missionary enthusiasts; but enthusiasts of the type that never grow weary in well-doing, and that will never be satisfied until the Master's own ideal is realized in the conversion of the whole world.

Our field of opportunity in Japan constitutes one of the greatest challenges presented to a Christian denomination by the non-Christian world. Two great circles of the native population, centering the one in Yokohama and the other in Japan, comprise each five hundred thousand people, giving an aggregate of one million souls; and all these by the common consent of Christendom left to the care of the Methodist Protestant Church!

Rev. Fred C. Klein, corresponding secretary-treasurer of the Board of Foreign Missions, was born in Washington, D. C. After the death of his father, the family removed from Virginia to Baltimore, where he attended the public schools. He at first entered upon a mercantile career, but after his conversion, under the pastorate of the Rev. L. W. Bates, D.D., and through the direct influence of his Sunday-school teacher, Mr. N. T. Meginniss, he yielded to the call, and entered Western Maryland College to prepare for the ministry, graduating from that institution in 1880.

For years he was impressed that he ought to be a foreign missionary, and that Africa would be his destination; but, at the call of the Board, he accepted the appointment as the first ordained missionary of our Church in the foreign field.

On his arrival in Yokohama, Dr. Klein started a night school; organized a day school for boys on the Bluff; organized the first church of the denomination in Japan; explored a large part of the main island for an interior location, this exploration leading him finally to settle upon Nagoya. He removed to Nagoya in 1887, opening the school there and beginning religious work, and later superintended the construction of the main building of the Nagoya College, becoming its first president, and the first president of the Japan Mission Conference.

Dr. Klein has been notably successful in his important work as corresponding secretary-treasurer. His rich experience in the missionary field, together with the prestige of great achievements in the Orient, prepared him at once for an intelligent farming of the churches in the interest of the great cause, and for the wise administration of the funds secured. Following in the path of great secretaries, his immediate predecessor being Dr. Tagg, the present incumbent has pushed forward and outward to meet the growing opportunities of the Church, and has accomplished with noble fidelity the expectations of our people and the ever-increasing demands of the missionary vineyard God has committed to the care of the Methodist Protestant Church.

In addition to the well-known missionaries already named, there are five men whom the Methodist Protestant Church will write on its every roll of honor. Rev. Dr. E. H. Van Dyke spent several years in Japan; and he got so near to the heart of the Japanese language as to have evolved a most interesting scheme for the simplification of that language; and this eager pursuit, together with his missionary activities, won the esteem of many

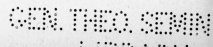

notables of the country. Rev. U. G. Murphy fulfilled
a most worthy career in Japan, accomplishing not only
the missionary task set him by the Board of Foreign
Missions, but initiating and achieving moral reforms that
won the attention and the approval of the Japanese Government. Rev. Leigh Layman, who still occupies the
field he has so faithfully tilled, has been honored with
the highest offices in the gift of the Mission and of the
Board, and has justified every confidence. Rev. Ernest
I. Obee, who has given the very flower of his life to the
foreign field, has been five years president of Nagoya
College, and has held, with many other positions of trust,
the chairmanship of the missionary parliament. Rev.
Charles S. Heininger, who presides over our important
mission field at Kalgan, China, has the reputation of having acquired a usable knowledge of the Chinese language
more quickly than any student of the period; and he
is doing the essential work of the mission, in its every
department, with the same unbounded energy and
efficiency.

WOMAN'S FOREIGN MISSIONARY SOCIETY

The Woman's Foreign Missionary Society of the
Methodist Protestant Church was organized in the First
Church, Pittsburgh, February 14, 1879. The organization of this important society was inspired by the presence of Miss Lizzie M. Guthrie, a returned missionary
from Japan; and she in turn had been ultimately led to
adore the Methodist Protestant Church through the
deep impression made upon her by the preliminary work
of our denomination in Yokohama.

The charter members of the Woman's Foreign Missionary Society are: Mrs. John Scott, Mrs. Susan E.
Anderson, Mrs. J. H. Claney, Mrs. Mary A. Miller,

Mrs. James I. Bennett, Mrs. N. B. O'Neil, Mrs. Martha Collier, Mrs. Eliza Sands, Mrs. J. J. Murray, Mrs. William Wragg, Mrs. William Barnhill, Mrs. A. Aughenbaugh, Mrs. William Wrighter and Mrs. W. K. Gillespie.

Rev. C. H. Williams, the Corresponding Secretary of the Board of Missions of the Methodist Protestant Church, attended the first annual meeting of the Woman's Foreign Missionary Society in Pittsburgh, and it was finally arranged that the Board and the Society should unite in sending Miss Guthrie to represent the Methodist Protestant Church in Japan. Miss Guthrie died soon after reaching San Francisco; but while her lamented death cast a shadow upon the missionary spirits of the whole denomination, the mantle of the departed handmaiden of the Lord fell upon Miss Henrietta G. Brittan, a woman of equal ability and devotion.

From these humble beginnings the Woman's Foreign Missionary Society has become one of the most progressive and efficient agencies of our denomination, having already sent twenty-six missionaries into the oriental field, while the home organization has, by rapid evolution, extended throughout the whole territory of the denomination, having led to the organization of eighteen branches, with three hundred and six auxiliaries and seven thousand three hundred and forty-three members. Beginning with the Pittsburgh Branch, which was organized in 1879, the work extended in the first year to the Muskingum, the Ohio and the Genesee, the Maryland following in 1881, the Missouri and the Iowa in 1882, and onward through the conferences up to the present time.

The report of the General Executive Treasurer, for the consecutive years beginning in 1879, is a very interesting exhibit of the constant progress and the ever widening scope of the work of the Woman's Foreign Missionary Society. The first report, forty years ago, shows an income of less than $400; but a fourfold increase is reported for the very next year, until the twenty-fifth anniversary discloses the receipt of more than $13,000, and the fortieth anniversary, more than $40,000.

The society has had five presidents from the beginning of its history: Mrs. Dr. John Scott, Mrs. F. A. Brown, Mrs. J. W. Gray, Mrs. E. C. Chandler and Mrs. Henry Hupfield; and five corresponding secretaries: Mrs. N. B. O'Neil, Mrs. Mary A. Miller, Mrs. J. J. Murray, Mrs. D. S. Stephens and Mrs. George H. Miller. The Executive Board of the Society as at present constituted is: Mrs. Henry Hupfield, Mrs. E. C. Chandler, Mrs. C. E. Wilbur, Mrs. Lida K. East, Mrs. J. E. Rhodes, Mrs. Andrew Lester, Mrs. George H. Miller, Mrs. S. W. Rosenberger, Mrs. P. W. Downs, Mrs. Clyde Barbe, Mrs. George Young, Mrs. William Sturgeon, Mrs. J. C. Ball.

The aim of the Woman's Foreign Missionary Society, as expressed by Mrs. Henry Hupfield and Mrs. George H. Miller in the quadrennial report of the Society at the last General Conference is: "To take the message of Christianity to the women and children of non-Christian lands." In the pursuit of this noble aim the Society is doing a well-established and progressive work in Japan, laying special emphasis upon Christian education and evangelistic work. The various schools under the auspices of the Society in Japan are overcrowded, and more room for the work and the workers is urgently needed. The Japanese field of endeavor is concentrated in three cities: Yokohama, Nagoya and Hammamatsu. The Society has a well-established home and kindergarten in Nagoya proper, and have now added to their work in that region a new enterprise in Atsuta, a suburb of Nagoya, the outlook of which is very encouraging.

During the past year the Society has greatly enlarged its sphere of work in China; and, while Rev. C. S. Heininger has been transferred to the Board of Foreign Missions, four women have been sent to Kalgan; namely, Miss Alice M. Shepherd, Mrs. Nelle Cairns Hurst, Miss Mabel Muller and Dr. Roberta Fleagle. Of these four, however, Miss Shepherd has been called from labor to reward, becoming a martyr to the cause of missions, and Miss Muller finds it necessary to return to America for recuperation.

Miss Donna Schlegelmilch is now conducting a department in the study of missions in Adrian College; and Miss Schlegelmilch is so thoroughly equipped for this work, both by her personal experience as a missionary in Japan and by her native talent and aptitude for the science of teaching, that this course of study becomes a splendid opportunity to the young people of the Methodist Protestant Church who may have dedicated themselves to life service for the Master in foreign lands.

The Methodist Protestant Church owes much of its success in the Orient to the aggressive energy and to the generous self-sacrifice of the Woman's Foreign Missionary Society. The early days of the organization were full of struggle, with innumerable incidents of a discouraging nature; but the faith and the zeal of these daughters of our Zion overcame all obstacles, and their phenomenal success during the last decade has been at once the result and the reward of their unwearied consecration to the sacred cause of Foreign Missions.

XIII

BEGINNING AT JERUSALEM

THE one text of Scripture which comprehends the two hemispheres of the world of missions is Luke 24:27: "And that repentance and remission of sins should be preached in his name among all nations, beginning at Jerusalem." The foreign missionary enterprise of the Christian Church responds to the requirement that the gospel of Christ shall be preached "among all nations." The home missionary movements of the Church respond to the equal requirement that this glorious ministry shall have its "beginning at Jerusalem."

When the apostles went forth, clad with the whole armor of God, and devoted themselves to the conquest of the world in the name of Jesus, they remembered Jerusalem first of all. This priority of claim in behalf of the metropolis of Israel was not based alone upon the fact that the Hebrews were the chosen people. The appeal of the gospel of Christ is ultimately a personal one; it goes straight to the individual heart. And the Lord commanded the disciples to begin at Jerusalem simply because that great city was peopled with the unsaved; and the gospel must go straight to every house, knock at every door, bring its heavenly message to every soul. In a word, Jerusalem was the first home mission field of Christian history; and from that day to the latest hour of the present age, the city which sends forth the gospel must itself be partaker of the Bread of Life. Every Christian community, like that group of disciples in the wilderness, is surrounded by a hungry multitude. The Christian Church has the loaves and fishes of the kingdom, blest and magnified by the miracle-working hands of Jesus. And the people who are in our own neighborhood, in our own city, in our own land, if they are still unfed in their spiritual natures, have the first claim.

Moreover, the disciples had found in Jerusalem the source of their power. In the Upper Room they learned to speak with other tongues; and all the hallowed memories of their spiritual coronation were associated with the city which first experienced the visitation of the Holy Ghost. And if, despite this divine advent, Jerusalem itself was still unsaved, surely it was important that the ministry of the disciples should have its beginning there. Every agency that goes abroad to the foreign field must look to the home field for its support, not alone in outward, financial things, but in all the manifold riches of wisdom and of grace. Therefore, the various influences and forces which are first of all bequeathed to the Christian community will go forth over the high seas and to the ends of the earth, and establish themselves thirty-fold, sixty-fold, an hundred-fold, in every dark continent, in every desert place.

For Methodist Protestants, the Master's injunction applies with an exact parallel of obligation. We are to preach the gospel to Japan and China, and to all people whom we can possibly reach with the divine message; but we must begin at Pittsburgh, at Baltimore, at Zanesville, at Columbus, at Chicago, at Greensboro, at Kansas City—at every center of influence, in all the borders of our Zion. For under the very droppings of our every sanctuary, even where our churches are planted in interdependent groups, in sympathetic touch one with another, there is, nevertheless, a home mission field. And, other things being equal, a group of three or five churches, already established, can plant an additional church in the same city, with half the effort and half the outlay that would be required in planting an additional church for the denomination in any isolated field. And the spiritual dearth requiring the new religious organization would be fully as great in the first instance as in the last.

And this "beginning at Jerusalem" carries its logic with equal force "into the next towns." Our first and greatest province in the empire of home missions is that of the growing American city, whether that city is east or west, north or south. But the same economy of spiritual forces which challenges the Methodist Protestants of every city to take their own town for God first of all, comes with an almost equal argument in favor of planting equal rights Methodism in the unoccupied territory of neighboring cities. We could move into Minneapolis all the more quickly because we are now in Chicago; and into Dallas, because we are already in Fort Worth, Paris and Tehuacana; and into St. Louis, because we are already in Indianapolis; and into Toledo, because we are already in Detroit, Adrian and Tiffin; and into Louisville, because we are already in Cincinnati; and into Portland, because we are already in Seattle; and into New Orleans, because we are already in Birmingham. There is a geographical factor in the problem of home missions; and, answering to this factor, there is a subtle, psychological factor, close up to the sacred offices of the

Holy Spirit. Jesus said: "Let us go into the next towns." The "next towns" could be reached more readily, they would be more responsive to the great message of his love, because they had already heard of his mighty works. The town or city which knows the very most about the mutual rights polity of the Methodist Protestant Church, that town or city is the most promising field for our home mission work; and the next best opportunity is to be found in that city which is hungering for mutual rights, and would gladly welcome, as from the very hand of God, such a system of church government as could offer at once the possibilities of liberty on the one hand and efficiency on the other.

The Board of Home Missions of the Methodist Protestant Church was organized at Grafton, West Virginia, July 24, 1888. Until that time the two hemispheres of missionary enterprise in our denomination had been administered under the one organization. The first president of the board was the Hon. F. H. Pierpont, the famous war governor of Virginia. Rev. Benjamin Stout, of the West Virginia Conference, was the first corresponding secretary, and his administration was fruitful of permanent results, in that he thoroughly organized the work, and established a number of home mission fields, giving himself with keen intelligence and prudent zeal to this new departure in our denominational life. The great war governor who served as the first president of our Board of Home Missions has nobly finished his earthly career, and the affectionate admiration of his countrymen is embodied in the heroic statue that stands in the hall of fame under the dome of the Capitol at Washington City. Rev. Benjamin Stout, the first secretary, still holds his place in the Lord's vineyard; and the consciousness of having launched, under General Conference authority, the cause of home missions in America for the Methodist Protestant Church, should be to him a happy remembrance and a sweet reward.

Upon the resignation of Dr. Stout, in 1897, the Hon. F. C. Chambers, a distinguished layman of Steubenville, Ohio, was chosen corresponding secretary; and, although his important business relations made it impossible to travel throughout the Church, Mr. Chambers conducted the affairs of the board from his own office in a wise and progressive manner, leaving a heritage of honorable achievement and of clearly balanced accounts to all who might succeed him. Having accepted this task, superadding it to his own important and exacting business, with the distinct understanding that he should be relieved by the next General Conference, Mr. Chambers retired at the close of the quadrennium, and was succeeded by Rev. G. E. McManniman, D.D.; and he in turn, at the end of five years, was succeeded by Rev. John H. Lucas, D.D., of the Pittsburgh Conference.

Under the aggressive leadership of Dr. Lucas, distinct and notable progress was made in the various fields of home-mission enterprise; and this efficient servant of the Church deserves credit in a special degree for the great improvement he wrought in the architectural standard of churches and parsonages erected during his term of office, and for the strategic nature of the sites chosen for new churches. One of his never-to-be-forgotten achievements in behalf of the Church was his management of the situation in Seattle, Washington, where, in the face of the apparent failure of our cause in that gate city of the Pacific, he turned the situation to good account for the whole denomination by disposing of the downtown property for one hundred thousand dollars, and reëstablishing the Church in its present dominating position on Capital Hill. Through this splendid piece of denominational strategy, Dr. Lucas launched the cause of democratic Methodism in that growing city on a new career of unbroken prosperity.

On the resignation of Dr. Lucas, in 1908, he was succeeded by Rev. C. L. Queen; and, after his brief career of two years, he was in turn succeeded by the present incumbent, Rev. Charles H. Beck, D.D., of the Ohio Conference; and Dr. Beck has been re-elected to this office by the General Conference of 1912, by the General Conference of 1916, and by the General Conference of 1920, receiving in each instance the unanimous vote of this highest court of the Methodist Protestant Church.

Dr. Beck is now completing the eleventh year of his administration of the affairs of the Board of Home Missions, and it is merely voicing the simple truth to say that this decade of endeavor in our home mission fields has witnessed the most notable achievements in the history of the board, and has been one of the chief accompaniments and, along with an equal revival in the field of foreign missions and in that of education, one of the chief sources of the progressive spirit which during the last few years has inspired the forward-moving ranks of the Methodist Protestant Church.

Among the mission enterprises which have engaged the energies of the board during these last progressive years, some of them having been newly launched, others continued, and still others carried on to self-support, are the following:

The University Church, the Chelsea Church and the

Gordon Place Church, in Kansas; the Squirrel Hill Church, Pittsburgh, and Philadelphia churches and Berwick, in Pennsylvania; Magnolia, Mansfield and other centers in Arkansas; Paris, Corsicana, San Angelo and Ft. Worth, in Texas; Hugo, Idabel, Comanche and Haworth, in Oklahoma; Paris, South Park, Canton and Avalon Park, Chicago, in Illinois; Keokuk, in Iowa; Kohoka, in Missouri; First Church, Ravenna Park and Sea View, Seattle, in Washington; White Plains, Hilburn and North Tarrytown, in New York; Moorestown and East Newark, in New Jersey; Stamford, in Connecticut; Greensboro, West End, Asheville and Charlotte, in North Carolina; Birmingham and Montgomery, in Alabama; Clarksburg and Grafton, in West Virginia; Adrian, Lansing, Flint and Detroit, in Michigan; Victory Memorial, Unity and Mansur Park, Indianapolis, and Logansport, in Indiana; Calvary, Trinity and Baltimore, in Maryland; Wilmington, in Delaware; Rhode Island Avenue, Washington, in the District of Columbia.

Rev. Charles H. Beck, D.D., the executive secretary of the Board of Home Missions, was born in Harrisville, Ohio, and resided in that village during all his boyhood days. He was converted and became a member of the Church at the age of sixteen, and his ministry in the Muskingum Conference, now the Ohio Conference, began in 1891. After sixteen years in pastoral work, during which he served a number of important charges with notable success, he was elected president of the Muskingum Conference, and continued in that office through five consecutive years, the full constitutional term of service; and during that period the splendid Conference Memorial Church at Zanesville was erected under his supervision by the joint effort of the conference and the congregation. The progressive mission work at Columbus, Ohio, was undertaken as a result of Dr. Beck's presidential initiative, and church-building, debt-paying and general progress were the rule throughout the whole conference district.

During the eleven eventful years of his connection with the Board of Home Missions, Dr. Beck has met the difficult problems of his important office with equal courage and ability. Possessing in large measure the vision of opportunity, he has been able to distinguish quickly the field of greatest promise for the kingdom of Christ and for the upbuilding of mutual-rights Methodism. In the financial management of the work of home missions, he has happily united the most rigid economy with the greatest possible efficiency; and the money of the Church under his care has gone farther and accomplished more than the average records of such an office are likely to duplicate. And during the last quadrennium, from 1916 to 1920, Dr. Beck has extended his sphere of service, with equal wisdom and fidelity, into another important field; for, at the urgent solicitation of the National Executive Committee, and after several distinguished laymen had declined the office, Dr. Beck was elected as the first general treasurer of the Methodist Protestant Church. The functions of this office included the receipt and disbursement of the Million-Dollar Campaign funds, together with all the manifold accounts of the various boards; and yet, notwithstanding his undiminished attention to the affairs of the Board of Home Missions, Dr. Beck dedicated time and talent in willing devotion to this new field of service; and the organizing genius he displayed in the initiation and development of this important office, as well as in the fidelity and accuracy with which he performed, from first to last, all the exacting functions of the office, challenges the grateful appreciation of the whole Church.

WOMAN'S HOME MISSIONARY SOCIETY

The Woman's Home Missionary Society of the Methodist Protestant Church became a distinct and independent organization in May, 1916, when the General Conference recognized the Society as an official unit of the Church apart from the Board of Home Missions. The women were formerly organized for the work of Home Missions in connection with the board; but since 1916 they have launched out in a larger way, and the Society consists, under its charter, of the General Executive Board, conference branches and auxiliaries of the local churches.

The Woman's Home Missionary Society is supporting a number of splendid enterprises.

The Children's Home at High Point, North Carolina, was the first great objective of the Woman's Home Missionary Society, the work having been initiated by the North Carolina Branch of the Society. The Children's Home is a monument to the aggressive enterprise of the women of the Methodist Protestant Church, and the whole denomination joyfully recognizes this great achievement in behalf of the children. The Children's Home is described elsewhere in this book under the title of "Special Institutions."

The Society is doing perhaps its greatest work at Pine Ridge, Kentucky, where Rev. and Mrs. Thomas R. Woodford are conducting at once a home and a school, under the auspices of the Society, for the mountaineers of all that region. The original plot of ground donated for the Pine Ridge school consisted of forty acres and two cottages but more recently a two-story building has been erected, containing four well-lighted rooms, including a chapel, three class rooms and a basement, in which is located the Manual Training Department. A second story was also added to the cottage, which is used as a girls' dormitory. An additional cottage of seven rooms has still more recently been purchased, together with an additional farm; and the whole property is valued at $15,000.

The Society established, in one of the foreign settlements of Pittsburgh, in 1916, a mission school, which has already accomplished good results, both for the people who are brought under the influence of the school and for the whole environment in which the school is located. This mission, being in the center of the largest mill district in all the world, is in touch with almost every nationality; and the work among them is fruitful of immediate results, but is greatest of all in its far-reaching possibilities. A resident social worker, and a number of assistants, are connected with the mission, and classes in domestic culture are assembled every day, while Bible training and a growing Sunday-school are a part of the Sabbath day activities of the mission.

The members of the Executive Board of the Woman's Home Missionary Society are:

Mrs. A. G. Dixon, President; Mrs. Jane A. Gordon, Corresponding Secretary; Mrs. E. A. Craig, Treasurer; Mrs. William C. Hammer, Miss Alice Conway, Mrs. Henry Hupfield, Mrs. H. E. Risler, Mrs. Paul Cullison, Mrs. J. O. Ledbetter and Mrs. A. P. Badger.

XIV

EDUCATIONAL MISSION OF THE CHURCH

THE future of this world, in all the centers of civilization, depends most vitally upon Christian education. And Christian education must continue to find its coherent voice in the Christian college. The public schools of America are important as factors of human freedom. They are for everybody, and the little red schoolhouse on the hill is at once the life of the neighborhood and the hope of the nation. But the religious atmosphere of the public school in our country has been impoverished, in many sections of the nation, by the removal of the Bible from its place among the books; and even the moral tone of the schoolroom has been lowered in this process, not alone by the absence of the divine standards of human life thus enforced, but by the spirit of indifference, if not of contempt, thus engendered in the minds of millions of young Americans for the moral authority of the Christian Church. The first impulsive conclusion of the child, when he sees the Christian's holy Book shut out of the daily reading exercises of the schoolroom, would express itself in some such inquiry as this: "If the Bible is forbidden to me in the school, where I am receiving all my lessons, then why should it be taught me in the home or in the Church?"

This battle of the Bible at the door of the public

school, and especially when the battle has resulted in the rejection of this text-book of the moral law, has done more harm in the hearts of our American youth than all the printed infidelity of the ages. The separation of Church and State is important to the cause of human liberty; and this recognized principle of our great republic forbids sectarian teaching in the public schools. But there is no sectarianism in the Bible itself. It is a book of universals, as broad in its revelations and doctrines as the empire of the soul. It is at once the morning star of the mind and the noonday sun of the heart.

But whether the public school admits the Bible or excludes the Bible, the turning point of millions of minds in this twentieth century is found within the golden circle of college life. Removed from the restraints of home, and deprived of the advice and influence of his pastor, the young man is plunged into an atmosphere which is all too often poisoned by the outspoken unbelief of other students. The trend of doubt is further encouraged by a sense of freedom; a certain pride of intellect which is readily fanned into vanity; the spirit of independence, rapidly growing into that inordinate self-consciousness which very often, instead of asking for the old paths, is swift to make paths of its own through the untrodden wilderness of speculation. Ah, how much the young man in such a mood, in such a crisis, needs the spiritual protection of a Christian college, wherein every science is so taught as to lead onward through every wilderness to the feet of God!

The Christian college is the hope of our country; and, just as in the past it has furnished a vast majority of the great public men of our nation, so in the future it must continue to send forth into the various channels of national life the men who will determine the destinies of the republic.

The educational institutions of the Methodist Protestant Church, while retaining their distinctively Christian character, have not become sectarian; nor have they made their moral ideals an apology for inefficient work in the purely intellectual field. They have given to the student the highest quality of service. To the best possible equipment in every department has been added that highest equipment of all, the ideal teacher; the teacher who, while he communicates to the student the things he ought to know, also gives himself to the student, thus exemplifying to him what he ought to be. No other denominational colleges in America have surpassed those of the Methodist Protestant Church in the high character and the splendid personality of their college professors. This fact stands out so clearly as to challenge dispute, whether we speak of our colleges historically, or in a contemporary way. Take them group by group, from the largest communions to the smallest, and our educators present an average which does not shrink from comparison with the best. At Adrian, at Kansas City, at Westminster and at Tehuacana; and at Westminster again, in the faculty of our theological seminary, we have men worthy of the unquestioning confidence of their own denomination and of the unreserved recognition of every Christian scholar in America.

THE BOARD OF EDUCATION

The Board of Education of the Methodist Protestant Church was constituted by the General Conference of 1916, this progressive event taking place at Zanesville, Ohio, one of the early centers of our denominational life. One of the chief functions of the new organization, that of seeking called and qualified candidates for the gospel ministry, had been hitherto exercised by the Board of Ministerial Education, this first organization having been formed some fifty years earlier than the second.

In the progressive evolution of a church, as of all institutions, outstanding men are the inspiration of outstanding events; and in the background of the Board of Ministerial Education looms, first of all, the heroic figure of Rev. James B. Walker, who was not only the real founder and father of this noble enterprise, but the one constant champion of the good cause from its earliest inception to the close of his great career in 1890. This royal pioneer in the kingdom of education invested twenty years of his life in the development of this denominational enterprise; and many of the leaders of to-day in our Methodist Protestant Church owe their larger success in the gospel ministry, not alone to the material help they received through the agency which he established, but also, in a still more intimate and sacred way, to the personal influence he used in persuading them to enter the ministry through the higher educational channels.

Second only to James B. Walker, and second only in course of time rather than in the measure of service rendered to the cause of ministerial education, stands that nobleman of the kingdom, Dr. James C. Berrien. For if James B. Walker was the Elijah of the school of the prophets for the Methodist Protestant Church, James C. Berrien was the worthy Elisha upon whom rested the prophet's mantle through many fruitful years. Dr. Berrien was peculiarly qualified, alike in moral temperament and in mental talent, for the delicate task of finding the way of approach to the hearts of young men, and of revealing to them the higher paths of duty. His sympathies were at once so keen and so cultivated that he possessed a real genius for communicating to others not only his own ideals and conceptions of the gospel ministry, but even his own spiritual vision, his own clear hope of final victory in every good fight of faith.

And, once upon a time, this unfailing optimism in the Lord's work made Dr. Berrien a special providence to Adrian College. A temporary embarrassment in the affairs of the institution had developed into a real crisis, and discouragement had for the moment paralyzed the hopeful energy essential to relief. In this crucial hour it was James C. Berrien who entered the arena, initiated an impromptu campaign, and, in a few days of enthusiastic endeavor, raised money enough to tide the ship over the shoals. Adrian College had many another friend and champion who would have leaped to the rescue before disaster had finally come upon the institution. But "honor to whom honor is due"; and it was James C. Berrien, and none other, who launched this noble and timely enterprise. And the memory of this service, together with other worthy achievements in his career of usefulness in the Church, must surely brighten the sick room down on Long Island where Dr. Berrien, even in his illness, still retains a keen and anxious interest in all that concerns the welfare of the Methodist Protestant Church.

The last of the educational secretaries of our Church under the old form of organization was Rev. Dr. George R. Brown. His term of service extended from 1908 to 1916; and during this double quadrennium he gave to the Methodist Protestant Church a wise and faithful administration of the educational funds committed to his care, while his accounts were a model of clearness and accuracy, and his whole career brought honor at once to himself and to the denomination.

The Board of Education, as organized at Zanesville in 1916, has general supervision of the whole educational field of the Methodist Protestant Church, still looking upon ministerial education, however, "as its most important work." And while the scope of service performed by the board, and even the measure of its official authority, is very broad, yet it does not contravene in any manner the vested functions of college trustees, nor trespass upon any of the zones of influence set apart to our several colleges. This board is intended to supplement, to help and to further every distinct and separate agency in our whole empire of religious education, and to correlate our colleges one to another, thus bringing them into mutual and vital sympathy, and bringing them also into harmonious service in the upbuilding of the educational standards of the denomination.

Rev. Dr. George H. Miller, the executive secretary of the Board of Education, has been the efficient and progressive leader of this larger educational movement in our Church since the day of its organization at Zanesville. Born at Dundee, Michigan, Dr. Miller graduated from Adrian College in the class of 1900; and in the fall of that year became pastor of the First Methodist Protestant Church of Steubenville, Ohio. He was recalled to that important charge sixteen consecutive years, and at each annual election was chosen by the unanimous vote of the congregation.

During his term of service the Church made phenomenal progress, the many activities of that period including the building of an ample and beautiful house of worship. At the end of the sixteen years, though having a unanimous call to remain in Steubenville, Dr. Miller accepted the secretaryship of the newly organized Board of Education; and his brilliant service to the Church in this capacity covers a manifold achievement.

First of all, he was required to carry out, through the official agencies involved in the transaction, the merger of the West Lafayette College with Adrian College. And in accomplishing this result he also conceived and consummated the plan of developing the West Lafayette College grounds and buildings into a Home for Aged Methodist Protestants. Another of Dr. Miller's notable achievements during his first quadrennium was the founding of a Student Loan Fund, "for the benefit of young men and young women of good character, who are high school graduates, and who will attend one of our own institutions of learning," a maximum loan of one hundred and fifty dollars being made to such students, without interest until graduation, and returnable with two per cent interest thereafter. This far-seeing policy has already made possible the realization of many youthful ideals; and, inasmuch as the plan was officially endorsed and established by the General Conference at Greensboro in 1920, the door of opportunity will open wide to hundreds of young men and young women who would otherwise be totally deprived of a college training.

In addition to all else, Dr. Miller has shown a peculiar genius for adequately meeting emergencies, and even for anticipating emergencies, in the educational affairs of the Church. The happy disposition of the college property at West Lafayette; the timely organization of the

Adrian College Six Hundred Club; a ready acquiescence in whatever readjustments were necessary to united action in the Million-Dollar Campaign; an instant and sympathetic response to every new requirement of our educational units, whether at Adrian or at Westminster, whether at Kansas City or at Tehuacana—these are but typical examples of the alert and constant attention this faithful secretary gives to the educational interests of the Methodist Protestant Church.

ADRIAN COLLEGE

Adrian College, the first institution of learning established by the Methodist Protestant Church, began its history in 1859, and became the property of our denomination in 1868. This college is the outgrowth of an earlier institution founded at Leoni, near Jackson, Michigan, in 1852. As a happy coincidence, Rev. Asa Mahan was at this time pastor of a Congregational Church in Jackson, and on his resignation from that field became pastor of the Plymouth Congregational Church in Adrian, Michigan. The suitability of Adrian as an ideal location for a college deeply impressed itself upon Dr. Mahan, who was one of Oberlin's early presidents, and a pioneer in the progressive development of co-education in America. The citizens of Adrian were responsive to this prophetic suggestion and appointed a committee to survey the situation and to inaugurate a movement for such an enterprise. The idea developed rapidly, and twenty acres of ground in the western part of the town were donated as a site for the prospective college, and $30,000 was quickly subscribed for the erection of buildings. In the meantime the leaders at Leoni were dissatisfied with their location and were prepared to take an immediate and practical interest in the offer made by the citizens of Adrian. The city finally agreed to take over the operation of the institution, and to raise $100,000 in five years for endowment, on the condition that Adrian should then become final owner of the institution.

At this juncture, however, the Wesleyan Methodist Church, under whose auspices the Leoni College was operated, had negotiated an organic union with the Methodist Protestant Church; and the Methodist Protestant Church had already organized a collegiate association centering at Springfield, Ohio, and having for its purpose the early founding of a denominational college. This proposed union was finally consummated, in so far as ecclesiastical legislation could bring it about; but the Wesleyan Methodists finally became backsliders on the question of church union, and but very few of their ministers and congregations actually entered into the new denomination known as the Methodist Church. This early object lesson in the failure of church union threatened for a time to defeat the arrangement for the transfer of Adrian College to the Methodist Protestant Church; and at one of the crucial points in the controversy, six Methodist Protestant Trustees resigned in favor of an equal number of the citizens of Adrian, but Adrian citizens themselves naturally grew weary of the vacillating policy of the Wesleyan leaders; and, inasmuch as the Wesleyan administration had failed to fulfill the conditions agreed upon at the time of the transfer, the Citizens Committee of Adrian demanded the instant fulfillment of the contract. This emergency prepared both the Wesleyan Methodists and the people of Adrian to turn over the college to any one church or interest which would assume the accumulated debt of $33,000 and endow the institution. The situation being therefore happily ripe for such a movement, the Methodist Protestant Church undertook the fulfillment of the required conditions and the college was transferred to a Board of Trustees comprising thirty members from the Methodist Protestant Church.

Since the founding of Adrian College, in 1859, by the joint-initiative of Asa Mahan and the citizens of Adrian, six thousand young people have been enrolled in her classes; and while indeed the majority of these students went out into the world before their course of study was finished, yet every true and yearning student among them found a noble legacy in Adrian College, and carried out from under the maples a light that shone afar on all the highways of life; and even many of those who remained but a few short months in these storied halls received a birthright which justified them in forever looking up to Adrian College as their true alma mater.

From the very beginning, and progressively with the passing years, Adrian College has maintained a high standard of scholarship. The educational authorities of America recognize the Adrian curriculum as one which is level with the best; and Adrian students at any starting point in the course of study can pass as readily to the next semester at the State University as to that of Adrian itself.

Adrian College is remarkable for the number of truly great administrators and teachers who have adorned and enriched her faculty. Among the educators who have given to the college long-time service of great value are Dr. Asa Mahan, at once a great teacher and a noted author who, after fulfilling the office of College President in a manner which gave him national distinction, laid down his burden fifty years ago, and whose name has been honored anew at Adrian through a special Mahan commencement; Adam H. Lowrie, who was the one great contribution of the Wesleyan Methodist College at Leoni, to the Methodist Protestant College at Adrian; Isaac W. McKeever, whose many years of scholarly service in Science Hall was accompanied with the noble qualities which made him equally popular with the student body and with the City of Adrian; George B. McElroy, who, even in his youth, was prominently identified with the earliest educational movements of our Church, and who gave to Adrian College the mathematical genius which deserved and received the recognition of the greatest mathematicians of America; Davis S. Stephens, whose long career at Adrian, as Professor and as President, was followed by an equally distinguished service as editor of the "Methodist Recorder" and as Chancellor of the Kansas City University; Charles Edgar Wilbur, for the last twenty years or more the well-known editor of our Sunday-school periodicals, who spent nine years at the head of the Department of English Literature, and exerted a lasting influence upon the minds and hearts of his pupils; J. F. McCullock, now editor of the "Methodist Protestant Herald," who was a most efficient professor at Adrian for many years and who crowned his career with two years as acting president; and Brayman W. Anthony, who gave ten busy and eventful years to the College Presidency.

Harlan Luther Feeman, now President of Adrian College, has distinguished himself with equal ability in four distinct fields of service: through a devoted and fruitful career as pastor of Pittsburgh Conference Churches; by his splendid service as Professor in the Westminster Theological Seminary, preceded by theological teaching in Adrian College, and by his brief but highly efficient service as Secretary of the Young People's Board. His presidential administration has won the hearty coöperation of every official unit of the Methodist Protestant Church, and the responsive sympathy and the practical support of the city of Adrian.

Other educators deserve honorable mention for notable service at Adrian College; but we have limited our list of names to those who have rounded out a distinct career at Adrian, and whose service has made their names a perpetual unit of influence in the college atmosphere. Two members of the present faculty have given long-time service of real distinction to the institution; namely, Professor Cornelius, whose name is honored for his works' sake throughout the denomination and the city, and Sarah J. Knott, who has been for many years the efficient and popular Dean of Women.

WESTERN MARYLAND COLLEGE

The Western Maryland College, like many of the greater institutions of the world, came into collegiate existence by progressive evolution rather than by any one act of organization. The educational unit out of which the college finally emerged was an humble private academy in Westminster, Maryland; and it became a college mainly because certain Christian citizens of that town had the vision to see the strategic location of Westminster both in its relation to the Methodist Protestant communities of the East and in relation to the general population of all that region. A rural city which stands halfway between the mountains on the one hand and great cities on the other is always, in every land, an ideal site for an educational institution.

This group of people sent a delegation to the Maryland Conference to petition for the adoption of the academy as a conference enterprise, and the Maryland Conference in turn, having adopted the suggestion, reported their action to the General Conference and received the approval of that highest court of the denomination.

But the Western Maryland College, operates, not directly through the General Conference of the Methodist Protestant Church, but under a charter from the state of Maryland through a Board of Trustees, this board being self-perpetuating.

The Western Maryland College has had two presidents of equal distinction in the educational world and in the arena of the Methodist Protestant Church. Rev. J. T. Ward, D.D., was president from the founding of the institution in 1867 to 1886, and he was succeeded by Rev. T. H. Lewis, D.D., LL.D., whose term of office extended from 1886 to 1920. Dr. Lewis was the first president of the Westminster Theological Seminary, even as Dr. Ward was the first president of the Western Maryland College; and when Dr. Ward retired from the presidency of the college to give place to Dr. Lewis, the future of both institutions was provided for by an interchange through which Dr. Ward became president of the Seminary.

The Western Maryland College presents to the eye a splendid group of buildings which are so arranged as to form an impressive architectural unit; and the long and brilliant administration of Dr. Thomas Hamilton Lewis as president of the Western Maryland is recognized as preëminently a building epoch in the history of the institution.

The grounds and buildings of Western Maryland College represent an expenditure of more than $450,000; but the phenomenal advance of property values during the last few years gives the institution real estate assets quite beyond the sum which expresses the first material cost of this educational plant.

The paid in and invested endowment fund of the Western Maryland College is now something over $200,000. And the institution has enrolled, during its history of fifty years, 3,731 students and has graduated 1,120.

Upon the retirement of Dr. Lewis from the presidency of the Western Maryland and his election to the presidency of the General Conference, he was succeeded in the college by Dr. A. Norman Ward, who comes to this larger mission with a splendid equipment for its manifold duties. Both in his former connection with the Western Maryland as vice-president, and in his brief but brilliant service as Chancellor of Kansas City University, he gave full proof of his educational ability. In his contact with the student body of a college he knows how to unite official dignity with that sympathetic fellowship which proclaims the teacher a friend, and which never fails to win, as a swift and sure reward, at once the highest respect and the warmest affection of those who gather about him in the classroom or encounter him on the campus. Whether in the educational or the ecclesiastical province of duty, his mind and heart always emerge from the narrow and provincial into the broader vision of the Kingdom of God. While, therefore, he is intensely devoted to every local obligation, he is also, in the true proportions of every situation, loyal to his denomination and to all the international and world-wide implications of the new age.

KANSAS CITY UNIVERSITY

The Kansas City University was established in 1894; and in so far as the personal equation can possibly enter into so great an enterprise, Rev. D. S. Stephens, D.D., LL.D., was the founder of this worthy institution of learning. Dr. S. F. Mather, of Kansas City, Kansas, a lineal descendant of Cotton Mather of Colonial fame, gave his entire estate to the Board of Trustees of the newly organized university, and thereby furnished the means essential to the enterprise. But the educational vision of Chancellor Stephens, combined with his intuitive recognition of the Mather farms as being a strategic location for a university, was the creative influence which brought about the final consummation of Dr. Mather's noble dream. Throughout his whole life Dr. Mather had cherished the hope of founding an institution of higher learning, and this high purpose, born in his heart while he was yet the child of poverty, still dominated his mind when the rapidly appreciating value of his property made him a man of real wealth. A Congregationalist, he cared more for Christian education than for denominational prestige, and therefore he became warmly responsive to the approach of Dr. Stephens, and these two lofty spirits became co-partners in the launching of this great enterprise.

Dr. Stephens was unanimously chosen as the first chancellor of the University, in 1894, and administered the affairs of the institution until 1914, when he was made chancellor-emeritus for life. This administration of twenty years brought innumerable burdens and anxieties to the new chancellor and his associates; but his un-wavering optimism, together with his undimmed vision of the future possibilities of the university, carried him triumphantly through every wilderness of doubt. And the founding of the Kansas City University becomes the crowning achievement of a career which included a term of years in the successful presidency of Adrian College, and a brilliant decade as editor of the "Methodist Re-corder," as well as bringing him the denominational recognition which made him four years president of the General Conference.

The late Henry John Heinz, of Pittsburgh, was, throughout all this epoch of beginnings, the constant and liberal friend of Chancellor Stephens, and of the university, and his generous response to the needs of the institution carried the enterprise over many a chasm; and there were crucial moments when, without his finan-cial help, the very life of the institution would have been sacrificed to its obligations.

In the year 1913 the Church of the United Brethren in Christ became co-partners with the Methodist Prot-estant Church in the ownership and administration of the Kansas City University, this agreement being brought about by the merging of Campbell College, at Holton, Kansas, a United Brethren Institution, with the Kansas City University.

In 1914 Rev. Dr. John H. Lucas was elected Chan-cellor of the University to succeed Dr. Stephens, and under his zealous and faithful administration great prog-ress was made both in the development of the institution itself and the removal of many burdensome obligations. Through the loyal coöperation of the Trustees of the institution, and a further gift of $25,000 by Mr. H. J. Heinz, together with a readjustment by which Mr. Heinz and other creditors accepted university lands in payment of the sum due them, Chancellor Lucas was enabled to remove the heavy funded debt of the institution.

After the lamented death of Dr. Lucas, Rev. A. Norman Ward, D.D., who had been for a number of years vice-president of the Western Maryland College, and who had clearly demonstrated his ability for effective work and progressive achievement in the sphere of higher education, was elected chancellor, and entered upon his task with the whole-hearted zeal which is characteristic of the man. Chancellor Ward not only projected still further the line of progress already laid by Chancellor Stephens and Chancellor Lucas, but pushed forward in new fields of endeavor, giving his attention very largely, however, to the solving of the financial problems of the university, and to the laying of broad plans for such an increase in endowment and equipment as would enable the university to realize her educational ideals.

Since the above lines were written, Dr. John Clark Williams has been elected Chancellor of the Kansas City University. Further reference to his notable career will be found under Westminster College. In his new field at Kansas City, Dr. Williams will have the hearty coöperation of other distinguished Methodist Protestants; notably, Professor S. S. Fisher who has compelled recognition as an American poet, and Professor William A. Robinson who has rendered most efficient educational service both at Adrian and at Kansas City.

WESTMINSTER COLLEGE

The only college of our denomination in the Great Southwest is located at Tehuacana, Texas, having been founded in 1895. The institution was first located at Westminster, Texas, and still retains the name of its birthplace. Rev. James Lisbon Lawlis, D.D., Rev. T. L. Garrison, D.D., Rev. F. W. Fagg, and Mr. Lycurgus Anderson, together with other associates, were the founders of this college. The chief honor for this enterprise, by the common consent of his co-workers, belongs to Dr. Lawlis. In 1896, Professor Charles Oscar Stubbs, A.M., was elected president of the College of Arts and Literature, while Dr. Lawlis continued as president of the School of Theology. The institution was moved to Tehuacana, Texas, in 1902; and after the death of Dr. Lawlis, which occurred in a few months after the re-location of the college, Rev. H. H. Price, A.M., D.D., was elected president of the School of Theology. In 1906, President Stubbs resigned, and the School of Theology was made a department of the college and Dr. Price was elected president.

In 1912 President Price resigned and was succeeded by Rev. J. C. Williams, A.M., D.D. Dr. Williams has presided over the destinies of the college during the last eight years and has won the grateful recognition of the whole Methodist Protestant Church because of his earnest, progressive and brilliant management of the affairs of the institution. He has been equally successful as a financial leader and as an educator; and our whole denominational territory, in a radius which extends through all the supporting conferences of the institution, has felt at once the helpful influence of his splendid Christian character and the cumulative force of his educational ideals.

Since the writing of the above lines, Rev. William Burton Sanders, A.M., B.D., for a number of years the efficient and popular dean of the institution, has become the President of Westminster College.

The college at Tehuacana has another value in addition to its purely educational worth. It has other functions, additional to those which are comprehended in the widest scope of educational work. Forming as it does the key to our denominational problem in the great Southwest, our Westminster College is the fortress of our home missionary enterprise in all that vast region; and upon the success and prosperity of the school depend, in a large degree, the success and prosperity of our every charge in the whole group of conferences in that section of the country. In the Texas Conference, now comprising all the territory of the former Texas Conference, and the Northwest Texas, there are a number of cities which present open doors of opportunity to our denomination. The genius of our Church is peculiarly adapted to the spirit of connectional independence which is characteristic of the spirit of the Southwest. The people in that region want cohesiveness, but they also want self-government; they want efficiency, but they also want freedom; they want progress, but they also want liberty. And all of this simply means that they are intensely American; and, in our conception of the matter, it also means that they are intensely Christian. We need only to enter in, with adequate forces, and possess the land which lies before us. And there are many strategic places in that region of the Southwest where our denomination is practically unknown, which would be immediately responsive to our approach; and a thousand doors of which it can be said to our denomination: "Knock, and it shall be opened unto you."

And in other conferences of the great Southwest there is an almost equal demand for the educational center now being established, under such favorable auspices, at Tehuacana. The Arkansas, the Louisiana, the Ft. Smith-Oklahoma, the Mississippi and the North Mississippi—all these have noble sons and daughters who will naturally look to this young and growing college for their educational opportunity. They are already in hearty coöperation with Texas in the support of the institution, and many graduates have gone forth from the halls of this alma mater to the professional callings in these districts. The people of the Southwest have made splendid investments in our Southwestern college; they have earned the right to expect from the north and the east enough help to finish the task which they themselves have so nobly begun.

The Methodist Protestants of North Carolina have for many years contemplated the founding of a denominational college in that state, and indeed heroic experiments have been made in that direction. But the present movement is accompanied with so many hopeful conditions, and is inspired at once by so great a degree of local pride and of denominational loyalty as to deserve and foreshadow the early realization of this noble project. If funds enough can be secured to establish such an institution on sure and lasting foundations, and if a strategic location is selected, the enterprise should be encouraged in every section of the Church. We have believed from the beginning, and our conviction deepens with every passing day, that the educational program of the Methodist Protestant Church will be strengthened, and her comprehensive ideal all the more quickly realized, by the building of a college in the great Southeast. Denominational colleges are interdependent, and when they are sufficiently multiplied to form a genuine family group, and when they are so wisely distributed as to put at least one denominational college within reach of every prospective college student in the whole territory of the Church, then, and only then, are we adequately equipped to meet the educational needs and opportunities of our people. A college in North Carolina will complete the educational circuit of the Methodist Protestant Church; and, just because such an institution will really complete the now broken circuit, every college in the denomination will be all the stronger because of this projected enterprise. Our college at Tehuacana, Texas, is a most valuable asset to the cause of democratic Methodism in the great Southwest; and the discontinuance of that institution, or the merging of its identity with that of any other educational unit, would be a great misfortune; a misfortune not alone to the section wherein it stands, but a misfortune to the whole educational composite of our denomination. Adrian College and the Kansas City University will be all the stronger for every onward stride in the development of our educational unit in the great Southwest, and the Western Maryland College will be all the stronger for every stone that is laid, literally or figuratively, in the walls of a new college in the great Southeast.

Since the above lines were written, the Methodist Protestants of North Carolina have conducted a whirl-

wind campaign for a new college, have raised by subscription hundreds of thousands of dollars, including a
single subscription of one hundred thousand by J. Norman Wills, and High Point has been chosen as the site
of the proposed college.

WESTMINSTER THEOLOGICAL SEMINARY

The Westminster Theological Seminary was established in 1882, the first Board of Governors being incorporated early in 1884. Rev. T. H. Lewis, D.D.
LL.D., was elected principal of the seminary by the
Maryland Annual Conference through the formative
period of the school, and was elected president of the
fully-established seminary by the Board of Governors
immediately upon their incorporation.   In 1886 Dr.
Lewis was succeeded in the presidency by Rev. J. T.
Ward, D.D., Dr. Lewis at the same time becoming president of the Western Maryland College.   On the death
of Dr. Ward in 1897, Rev. Hugh Latimer Elderdice,
A.M., D.D., was elected to the presidency, and has continued this important leadership during all the years
since then, fulfilling a career unsurpassed in its fidelity
to the Methodist Protestant Church and to the kingdom
of God, and so eminently successful that the denomination is enriched with the ministry of some two hundred
graduates of the seminary.

Dr. Elderdice has three associates in the faculty who
are well known throughout the whole Church: Rev.
Charles Edward Forelines, A.B., D.D., Rev. Montgomery J. Shroyer and Rev. Herbert Taylor Stephens,
A.M., D.D.

The call to the ministry, in every dispensation of the
God of Israel, has been first a call to preparation.   Even

the Son of Man, though he was also the Son of God, was called to the study of the books before he was called to the preaching of the word! Yea, his whole life, save only the last three years, was one of preparation. And the glorious consummation of that wonderful life was the foreordained sequel of the times of preparation. Three years of achievement; twenty-seven years of preparation! For he went to the school of the home, down in Nazareth, learning the wisdom of obedience; and to the school of the synagogue, learning the wisdom of the law and the prophets; and on to higher schools, which we know not of, until the fullness of the time for the proclamation of his Messiahship, and for the beginning of his world-wide shepherding of the souls of men.

What glimpses of the books and of the schools we catch between the silent, unwritten years of the life of Jesus! "And it came to pass that after three days they found him in the temple, sitting in the midst of the doctors, both hearing them and asking them questions." Even when the door of mystery closes upon him at Nazareth, the long interregnum is covered by this Scriptural assurance: "And Jesus increased in wisdom and stature, and in favor with God and man." When the door of revelation opens again, we find the Son of Man going to the preparation of the wilderness, to the school of temptation; after which we have this still further testimony to his preparation among the books: "And he came to Nazareth, where he had been brought up, and, as his custom was, he went into the synagogue on the Sabbath day and stood up for to read." Whereupon he proceeds to preach an expository sermon which evidenced the deepest familiarity, not alone with the Scriptures, but with the ultimate secrets of human nature. Yes, Jesus himself, the rabbi supreme, doubtless appropriated all the schools of his day to the human development of his mind and heart, thus multiplying and widening the windows of sympathy through which he might look out upon the world which he had come to save; which he had come to save not only from moral degradation and from the death that never dies, but also from those intellectual errors and sophistries which, in every age, are at once the source and the product of sin.

Every man who is called to the ministry of the gospel must enter, first of all and last of all, the school of Christ, and surrender both mind and heart to the fashioning influence of the Divine Teacher; must open all doors to the incoming of the Holy Spirit, who, in accordance with the Saviour's promise, is forever waiting to lead both pastor and people into all truth. But the Church is commissioned of God to teach her own children; and those who are to become the undershepherds of the flock of Christ are in need of every possible aid in preparation for their great work. Theological seminaries are the chosen means of instruction for those who are called to the ministry; and our own denomination is highly favored in the possession of such an institution as the Westminster Theological Seminary. The instruction given there, under the direction of President Elderdice and his associates, is progressive, thorough and comprehensive, keeping step with modern scholarship in every province of human thought, and yet humbly asking for the old paths wherein is the good way. The young man who goes to Westminster will find that the citadels of his faith are not to be assailed there by the wavering opinions of the mere explorer, but guarded at every gateway by the established convictions of an evangelical Christianity.

Friday, December 17, was a high day in the annals of the Westminster Theological Seminary, for that was the time set apart for the dedication of the splendid new building henceforth to become at once the school and the home of Methodist Protestant students for the gospel ministry.   President Elderdice and his associates in the faculty, with the hearty coöperation of the loyal friends of the institution in the various annual conferences, have looked forward joyfully to this occasion, and the final consummation of the enterprise was the only reward they desired in return for the arduous labors of the long financial campaign.   The new seminary building, because of the wise economies practiced under the able administration of President Elderdice, and because of willing-hearted service rendered by those who followed the noble example of the faithful Israelites in the making of the tabernacle, represents an expenditure of approximately one hundred and twenty-five thousand dollars; but, expressed in terms of the present-day value of building material and labor, it stands for at least two hundred thousand dollars.   It is a building of rare beauty, having the proportions that make it a veritable gem of architecture, with a degree of repose that happily suggests the true foundations of the Church, and presenting at once the appearance of a temple of learning and a sanctuary of the faith.

XV

THE YOUNG PEOPLE'S ERA

THESE progressive times have been called the age of steam, the age of electricity, the age of invention, the age of combination; and the miracles of civilization which have been wrought in this era have been attributed, in some descriptive phrase, to every factor of social evolution. But, if we would attribute results to their human agencies, in any collective way, we must simply call this epoch of ours the Young People's Era. For the past fifty years, the young man has ruled the market-place. The familiar adage, "Old men for counsel and young men for war," has lost much of its meaning; because the whole arena of life, including business as well as politics, has become so much a warfare that the world only feels the need of young men for war. Youth is at the helm on every sea, guiding the ship of state, the ship of commerce and even the ship of Zion! Perhaps it might be said that, beginning some twenty-five years ago, this Young People's Era was peculiarly manifest in the Christian Church, the movement finding rapid and fruitful expression and realization in the Young People's Society of Christian Endeavor, an organization which has achieved, above every other glorious result, the reawakening of the people of God.

And the moral revival in American politics and business, in these very times of ours, must be attributed

largely to the fact that the first generation of Christian
Endeavorers has now come into possession of its own
great proportion in the affairs of the world.   Spiritual
forces are the most indestructible of all forces; and the
spiritual energy which, ten and twenty years ago, found
voice in the religious function of testifying for Christ,
is now finding voice in the moral regeneration of our
cities, our institutions, our ballot-box, our whole body-
politic.

There were those who feared the possible result of
the Young People's Era, being persuaded that while the
world clamored for the energy of youth in the various
activities of life, the counseling wisdom of age and experience might be ignored and forgotten.   There was
indeed a momentary danger of such a result.   Perhaps
it should even be admitted that, in a passing and transitory way, this fear was unhappily realized, and that the
venturesome and speculative passion of the world's
market-place in these last years arose largely from the
unfortunate absence of the experienced elders of the
land in the various activities of business, of politics and
of religion.   But in the final result, this tendency has
disappeared, and the Young People's Era, as an ultimate
influence, has made the whole world young again!   For
a time, men talked of the dead-line in the ministry; and
as to efficiency in the world of business, they set the limit
absurdly low in the measure of the years.   Men in the
very prime of life, strong in mind and body, and crowned
with the ripe and rich experience so manifestly needed in
the management and execution of the world's work, were
rudely thrust aside.

But the reaction has come; not a complete reaction,
but just enough to leave the world in a more healthful

state, morally and physically, than it has ever known before. How was this result attained? It was attained by the rejuvenation of old age itself, so that the Young People's Era now belongs to everybody, from the Junior Endeavorer to the grayest of the gray in all the Brotherhood! When men discovered that old age was no longer in the market, they ceased to grow old! And as the world looks upon itself to-day, in the mirror of the new philosophy of life, the genuine Christian philosophy of life, the world sees a new and happy face. And in this new vision of youth, there is a great miracle of achievement for the kingdom of God, ripe and ready for realization.

The Board of Young People's Work of the Methodist Protestant Church was organized at the Pittsburgh General Conference in 1908, and Rev. Charles H. Hubbell, D.D., was elected general secretary of the Board. Dr. Hubbell was already a man of large experience in young people's work, having been secretary of the Young People's Union of the state of Ohio, and his selection was an earnest of the success of the enterprise. No provision was made at this General Conference for the financing of the Board, but the genius of Dr. Hubbell for the work to which he was assigned, and his unfailing optimism, carried to the pitch of enthusiasm for the good cause, led the organization to almost immediate success. A number of leaders had looked upon this venture as a mere experiment, and many doubts were expressed as to the successful development of the work, but before the quadrennium had passed away the new Board had so well justified itself that the General Conference of 1912, at Baltimore, fully adopted this youngest member of the official family, and reëlected

Dr. Hubbell with many well-deserved tributes to the efficiency of the service he had rendered to the denomination.

After the lamented death of Dr. Hubbell in 1914, Rev. Harlan L. Feeman, D.D., was elected to succeed him, and he served the Church faithfully and efficiently in this capacity until the summer of 1917, when he was called from the Young People's Work to the presidency of Adrian College. It was then that the present secretary of the Board of Young People's Work, Rev. A. G. Dixon, of High Point, North Carolina, was called to lead the forces which had been so happily organized by Dr. Hubbell and so splendidly led onward by Dr. Feeman. Dr. Dixon was called from the pastorate of the First Methodist Protestant Church at High Point, and he had already made a splendid career in the pastoral field before he was promoted to General Conference service. Dr. Dixon is a man of consecrated enthusiasm and is richly endowed, both in mind and heart, for the department of the kingdom to which he has been called.

Under the administration of Dr. Dixon the work of the Board has steadily grown in favor not alone with the young people themselves but with the conference leaders throughout the denomination and with the people as a whole. The work has been organized under seven departments, with a superintendent for each department:

1. The children's work.
2. Young people's work.
3. Adult work.
4. Teacher training.
5. Christian stewardship.
6. Missions.
7. Sunday-school architecture.

Already there are fifteen conference unions in as many annual conferences. These unions have their officers and also superintendent for each of the departments, corresponding with the department under the general work. The Young People's Work is not over-organized, as modern societies and enterprises too often are these days; but the machinery is at once simple and sufficient to accomplish the best results. The work is of course circumscribed in some degree by the fact that the workers are volunteers and can only give to the functions of their several offices such time as they can spare from their regular occupations. Besides the regular denominational conventions being held at stated intervals, under the auspices of the Board, the several conference unions have planned and realized a summer school of methods in each' of the several conferences in connection with the young people's conventions. These various schools have already accomplished good results and have been the source of great inspiration to the young people in attendance, and already the Church is beginning to reap many golden sheaves as a result of the seed-sowing by Secretary Dixon and his able assistants in the school of methods.

The scope of the work of the Young People's Board is such as to include both religious education and evangelism, this work being done through the agency of the Sunday-schools and the Christian Endeavor Societies. And while trying to perform this task the young people and their leaders took a very active and fruitful part in the forward movement which culminated in the victory campaign of the last quadrennium.

The departmental superintendents are as follows: Children's Work, Mrs. H. W. Maier; Young People's

Work, Professor M. J. Shroyer; Adult Work, Rev. E. D. Stone; Teacher Training, Mrs. A. G. Dixon; Missions, Rev. T. M. Gladden; Christian Stewardship, Rev. Roby F. Day; Sunday-school Architecture, A. G. Lamont. These superintendents are rendering splendid voluntary service to the great cause, but Mrs. Maier, superintendent of Children's Work, has for many years devoted herself so entirely to this field of service as to deserve a word of special recognition. Pearl Smith Maier is a real genius, both in method and manner, for ministry to the children and the young people of the Church; and her plans are truly workable in every section and corner of the denomination.

XVI

SPECIAL INSTITUTIONS

HOME FOR AGED METHODIST PROTESTANTS

THE Methodist Protestant Church was comparatively late in entering the humanitarian field of Christian enterprise, but during the last eight years, under the auspices of the General Conference, supplemented by a number of the Annual Conferences, the most encouraging progress has been made in this direction. The Home for Aged Methodist Protestants, at West Lafayette, Ohio, comes to our denomination as a special providence, and is already realizing, in many ways, the ardent hopes of those who rejoice in its noble purpose.

The buildings now constituting the Old People's Home, at West Lafayette, were formerly known as the West Lafayette College. But after fulfilling a brief but worthy career in the province of education, this college was merged with the oldest college of our denomination at Adrian, Michigan. As the first step in this procedure, the General Conference of 1916 took over the educational property interests of the West Lafayette College, making it thereby a denominational possession. The newly organized Board of Education was at the same time empowered by the General Conference to adjust at once all the holdings and all the obligations of the college. This adjustment having been made, the question naturally arose: "What shall be done with the buildings and grounds at West Lafayette? Can the denomination, having provided for the incumbrance on the property, turn that property into a channel of immediate usefulness to the whole Church, and a use so high and noble as to make it a new source of enthusiasm to the Methodist Protestant Church?"

Dr. George H. Miller, the secretary of the Board of Education, suggested the adaptability of the West Lafayette property for a Methodist Protestant Old People's Home. In response to the suggestion, after its adoption by the whole Board of Education, the Executive Committee at its special session in June, requested the presidents of those annual conferences forming the inner circle around West Lafayette, to visit the site and to report their findings to the regular meeting of the Executive Committee in Columbus. Five of the presidents visited West Lafayette, and their report was so favorable that the Executive Committee endorsed the project and advised the Board of Education, acting upon the full authority already vested in it by the General Conference, to announce to the Church this large and worthy purpose concerning the property at West Lafayette. With its substantial and home-like buildings, with its beautiful surroundings and its healthful environment, the splendid site makes an ideal home for the aged of our denomination; and so happily supplements, both in location and in purpose, the Children's Home at High Point, as to combine these two institutions in the one appeal to the loftiest humanitarian sentiments of the Methodist Protestant Church.

The property of the Old People's Home is worth at least fifty thousand dollars, and the general environment of the Home is such that it will appreciate in value through the years, even without reference to the development of the property itself. Already the main building, known in college days as Orchard Hall, has been thoroughly modernized and adapted in every way to the purposes of the Home; and, as a rare and delightful advantage, a water tank has been reared, through which the waters of a perennial spring, in the hillside above the orchard, are distributed throughout the building, thus adding still another factor to the natural healthfulness of the Home. There still remain four other buildings, all of which readily lend themselves to the supreme object of the Home, while the town of West Lafayette itself is at once near enough for ready approach by the residents of the Home, and far enough removed to give to the Home itself all the advantages of a rural atmosphere. The outlook from Orchard Hall discloses one of the typical beauty spots of Old Ohio.

The main conditions for admission to the Home, put in the briefest terms, are these: Applicants shall be sixty-five years of age, or over; must have been members of the Methodist Protestant Church for ten years prior to the application; must turn over to the corporation, previous to their admission, any property which they may possess, or which they may later acquire; must serve a probation of six months before being admitted to permanent residence; those having no property received as residents for life on the payment of $500; any departure from these conditions to be made only by a concurrent vote of two-thirds of the members of the Board of Trustees.

The members of the Board of Trustees of the Old

People's Home are as follows: Rev. J. W. Hawley, Rev. M. R. Stover, Rev. E. T. Howe, Rev. C. C. Falkenstine, Mr. H. A. Sicker.

CHILDREN'S HOME

The corner stone of the Children's Home at High Point, North Carolina, was laid with proper ceremonies October 17, 1912. But even before the site of this institution had been chosen on that consecrated forty acres, the institution itself had a sure foundation in the faith of its promoters, and a realizing force in their loyal enthusiasm. A number of the founders of the Home have already passed from labor to reward, including Professor H. M. Holt, who was master of ceremonies at the corner stone laying; Mr. T. A. Hunter, who was chairman of the finance committee; Dr. J. R. Reitzel, who was from the beginning a leading spirit in the noble enterprise, and Mr. and Mrs. J. J. Welch, who contributed the original site for the Home, and who gave liberally, apart from this splendid donation, toward the building of the Home itself. But they being dead, yet speak a noble language; and the Children's Home becomes, in a most beautiful sense, the lasting and living monument to those who gave so largely of their abundance and of themselves to the noble enterprise. Mr. J. M. Millikan, who has been chairman of the Board of Trustees from the very beginning, is still occupying the same responsible position, and is fulfilling every obligation with loyal devotion to the great cause, and with a far-seeing wisdom in every province of the worthy enterprise.

At the corner stone laying Professor H. M. Holt was master of ceremonies, and met all the demands of the occasion with ready tact and rare ability. The following persons took part in the ceremonies:

Mr. T. A. Hunter, chairman of the Finance Committee; Hon. F. N. Tate, mayor of the city of High Point; Mr. J. J. Fariss, editor of the "High Point Enterprise"; Rev. Dr. T. J. Ogburn, pastor of the Greensboro Methodist Protestant Church; Rev. Dr. W. E. Swain, president of the North Carolina Conference; Mrs. W. C. Hammer, of Asheboro, the leader of the noble band of women who inaugurated the Children's Home; Dr. J. R. Reitzel, chairman of the Building Committee; Mr. J. M. Millikan, chairman of the Board of Trustees; Mrs. A. G. Dixon, denominational agent for the institution; Rev. Dr. J. C. Broomfield, a member of the Board of Trustees, and Rev. Dr. Lyman E. Davis, president of the General Conference.

The humanitarian sentiment and the Christian enthusiasm which originated the Children's Home arose in the hearts of the North Carolina Branch of the Woman's Home Missionary Society, and these consecrated women, with the instant and loyal support of the North Carolina Conference itself, took the first step toward the founding of the institution. The Home was later indorsed and adopted by the Woman's Home Missionary Society of the whole denomination; and although the institution is now under the direct control of the General Conference, and is in all respects a denominational enterprise, the various branches of the Woman's Home Missionary Society make the support of the Children's Home one of the factors of their annual budget, so that contributions are received and welcomed from every conference and congregation of the Church.

The Children's Home at High Point is adorned by

one of the most substantial and beautiful buildings, for its purpose, in all the land. Standing on a slight eminence, looking toward the city of High Point on the one hand, and toward the mountains on the other, and surrounded by a farm which is rich-soiled and fruitful, this building is one of the progressive landmarks in the onward history of the Methodist Protestant Church.

The Home is not alone a refuge for the orphan children of our denomination, but is also one of the most efficient schools within the bonds of the Church, the farm providing the industrial school for the boys, while the daily routine of the Home includes the well organized school for both the boys and the girls, which covers in a thorough way the various primary branches; and the lessons here taught are so well learned as to make this school one of the distinct educational units of the Methodist Protestant Church.

XVII

DEVELOPMENT OF COUNTRY CHURCHES

THERE is in America to-day a great rural awakening, with the country church as the center of a new influence. This happy and progressive movement is associated with the effort to stem the tide of population which has flowed for generations from the country to the city, and to create and direct an healthful counter-movement from the city to the country. The telephone and the interurban railway have been great material aids to this revival of interest in country life, but it has come largely from a genuine growth of popular intelligence; an awakening of fathers and mothers to the importance of a rural atmosphere and environment for their children; a broader social comprehension of the moral dangers of the city, with a commensurate appreciation of the moral value of God's vast out-of-doors, as a determining influence upon the world's childhood; and a discernment of the art of prevention in moral reform, both in relation to the child and the immigrant, on the part of social philosophers and Christian teachers.

The rural church movement is simply the religious expression of the new era in country life. The progressive country neighborhood demanded the progressive country church. The progressive pastor, making his advent into these new conditions, has given himself, in many communities, to the development of the country church along the lines adapted to the needs of the people.

And in many instances the pastor has established the progressive country church even before the neighborhood was itself awake to the new movement. He has made the re-awakened country church the one supreme influence for the revival of the neighborhood to all its forgotten functions. But whether the country pastor and his church have been the forerunners in the movement or only the willing and intelligent servants of the new age they were keen enough to see that the main purpose of the rural church movement is to make the country church the center of life and influence to the whole community, to the farthest reaches of its possible influence; to make the Church the social center of the neighborhood as well as the religious center; to assume the position of friend and monitor to every man, woman and child in the community; to save not only the soul unto salvation and immortality, but to save the husband to the home, the citizen to the state, the man to humanity; to have a sympathetic eye to all the manifold interests of the people, making all questions that concern their material welfare a part of the Church's mission and the Church's prayerful anxiety, even to the kind of bridges that span their creeks and rivers, the kind of fruits they grow in their orchards and vineyards, the kind of books they read, the kind of amusements they enjoy, the kind of life they live.

The Methodist Protestant Church, like all the evangelical denominations of America, has always given a great proportionate share of attention to the country church. In our earlier history, the country church absorbed the energies of our people almost to the exclusion of the claims of the city, notwithstanding the fact that our denomination had its birth in the town. During the first two generations of our Church history, we needed especially to follow the Saviour's example by going "into the next towns." The country church was the principal unit of the annual conference; the circuit was the vineyard of early Methodism, and the circuit-rider was the Christian hero of the times. And the country church of that period was the center of the community's life, to an extent as great as the ideals of the country church movement can possibly realize. But the country life of that period was not as complex as that of to-day, and the demands of the rural neighborhood were not so great. In these days, our Methodist Protestant Church is everywhere making almost equal progress in town and country; and its progress in this respect is well-proportioned and symmetrical. We need, however, in common with all denominations, a broader comprehension of the Church's mission, whether in the city or the country-side; a realization of the fact that the Church must concern itself with the whole problem of human life, developing plans of organization and of personal ministry which will include the whole family unit, and all the factors of environment which affect in any manner the destinies of the people, whether they have "joined the church," or belong rather to that innumerable company that stands aloof awaiting the intelligent and sympathetic approach of the servants of him who said: "Go ye out into all the world, and preach the gospel to every creature."

It must of course, be remembered, and it will be remembered, that after all the one supreme mission of the country church, as of the city church, is the preaching of the gospel, and the subservience of every agency to the conversion of souls. Our leaders in this new movement are not eccentric; they are not disposed to develop the social functions of the Church to the exclusion of the spiritual; they are not forgetful of their greatest commission. Indeed, both in theory and practice, the progressive country church has abundantly justified itself. Conversions have multiplied with other units of progress, and the social awakening of the community has accompanied a moral and spiritual awakening.

Many of our country pastors, supported by loyal and liberal congregations, have entered heartily into the work of developing their country charges into genuine community centers. We can say without exaggeration that the Methodist Protestant Church at Harmony, Missouri, under the pastoral care of Rev. C. R. Green, has become justly famous for its progressive and comprehensive work in organizing the community in which it is situated. A few years ago, the little cross-roads neighborhood known as Harmony had its little cross-roads chapel; and, like the thousands of rural congregations of every creed, the good people of that out-of-the-way appointment did not think of any unusual possibilities in the direction of social betterment. And perhaps the last of all things within their field of vision would have been that of the Church itself as an agency of social development. The Church was the place of prayer, and only the bread of the spiritual man could be broken there! The very idea of making the Church the center of the social life of the community would have been condemned as secular and worldly, to the very pitch of sacrilege! And who dreamed that the Harmony Church would ever, on its own account, go into the business of road-making, or of scientific farming, or of finding out how to do the things of the world in a wise and profitable manner?

And even now, let us hasten to say, the Harmony Church does not sacrifice its religious heritage to its social ideals. It has never for one moment neglected the spiritual needs of its neighborhood. The real secret of this marvelous development at Harmony is to be found, as we believe, not primarily in the social aims and ideals of pastor and people, but in the old-time religion of their hearts; that religion seeking, however, the larger expression of itself in bringing happiness to the home, fruitfulness to the orchard and the field, improvement to the farm buildings and their environment, and a unity of purpose to the whole neighborhood.

The parish of the Harmony Church, as surveyed by Rev. C. R. Green, comprises twenty-three and one-half square miles, and within that territory there are something over five hundred people, all of whom are living on farms. There is no grouping of houses anywhere in all the parish which would suggest in the remotest way the country hamlet. They are farmers, and farmers only; and are justly proud of the genuine rural development which has been brought about through their efforts. The author was there at one of the recent annual home-comings; and, despite the heavy rains of the morning, three thousand people came to the services of the afternoon, while even in the morning, only an hour after the rain had ceased, the church was filled to the doors, all seating room in the aisles was occupied, and there was another audience of equal proportions who could not gain entrance to the building.

The pastor and people at Harmony have done a great work for their community and for the Methodist Protestant Church, and they have elevated the civic standards of their country. No wonder the fame of this movement has gone abroad throughout the whole state, and into regions beyond.

Another important community center service in our denomination is that initiated a few years ago by Rev. W. E. Grove, a member of the Ohio Conference, and later an efficient religious worker overseas in the Great War. Rev. Mr. Grove has been for many years an experimental student of the rural church problem, and served for a time as denominational superintendent of the Country Life Department of the Methodist Protestant Young People's Union. With his ideal clearly before him, and a thorough acquaintance with the nature of his task, he became pastor of two federated churches in northern Ohio, one at Old Fort and the other at Shiloh. The federation of these two churches for community center work was also an interdenominational experiment; for the Old Fort Church is a United Brethren appointment, while the Shiloh Church is Methodist Protestant. The ideals and standards pursued in the two places were identical, but while the work of the Sunday-school was featured especially at Old Fort, the Shiloh Church was developed, with intensive energy, along the lines of community betterment.

In a letter to the "Methodist Recorder" of January 9, 1915, Rev. W. E. Grove expressed the final spiritual purpose of his work in these two churches in this one forcible sentence: "Our task is to capture the whole community life, and the community's whole life, for our Friend and Saviour Jesus Christ." Rev. Mr. Grove was true to this noble aim; and while he developed with unusual energy the social functions of the community, he never lost sight of his own motto.

Other pastoral leaders of our denomination have done

heroic work and performed lasting achievements in this field of service.

Rev. E. N. Comfort, now a well-known professor in our Westminster College, Tehuacana, Texas, developed an interesting and helpful community center work at Union Church, North Illinois Conference, while he was pastor of that charge, a few years ago.

Rev. Dr. R. B. Whitehead, who was once pastor of our Trinity Church, Brooklyn, New York, and later pastor of a number of important charges in the Pittsburgh Conference, established many features of the community center church at Orange, Ohio.

Rev. R. E. Brooks, a promising young man of the Ohio Conference, is now pastor of the Shiloh Community Church, and is successfully developing the work so auspiciously begun by Rev. W. E. Grove.

Rev. J. L. Nichols, of the Maryland Conference, has studied rural church life for many years, and in an article to the "Methodist Recorder," entitled "The Country Church," he tells the following story of his own experience, and in the telling discloses in a vivid manner the psychology of the boy at his moment of decision between town and country.

"Why do the young people wish to leave home and go to the city?

"There are two ends to the answer. The country end is this: 'The parents, in almost every case, where the brightest children go to the city, are living on tradition, and insist, in the face of changed conditions all around them, on treating the children as they were treated and giving them only such advantages and privileges as they had.' There is really a reason for this, and that reason is the fact that this country is now in the midst of a great agricultural evolution and these parents are not keeping up with the times."

The Methodist Protestant Church has welcomed every helpful survey of country churches, and has tested, even by anticipation, many of the suggestions made by the modern leaders of the rural church movement. The author desires to say in this connection three things based upon a sympathetic study of this whole problem:

1. The Federated Church, when formed by the union of congregations long established in the community, often intensifies denominationalism instead of developing permanent coöperation; and for this and various other reasons, the Federated Church uniformly results in ultimate failure.

2. When alternative methods of consolidation are employed, such as the absorption of one denominational unit in another, both wisdom and honor require that the initiative shall be taken by the proper denominational leaders, and not by extra-denominational dictators.

3. Every denomination, every pastor, every religious survey, should sit in judgment upon all artificial approaches to the problems of the Kingdom of Christ, whether in town or country. For in all too many of the movements that assume to be progressive, we hear only the noise of the wheels, rather than the "sound of a going in the tops of the mulberry trees."

XVIII

METHODIST PROTESTANTS IN THE GREAT WAR

THE Methodist Protestant Church has always been the champion of liberty and self-government, and her people were enlisted in the Great War from the moment the Stars and Stripes appeared in the long battle line. It is impossible, however, to make a complete survey of the war-time activities of our denomination. The patriotic beneficence of our people found expression very largely through direct personal gifts to various national agencies, through the war chest of separate communities and through various interdenominational channels; and, while the unstinted offerings of our people often lost in this manner their sectarian identity, we believe they have been for that very reason all the more a blessing to the cause of freedom and humanity.

But we are prepared to name certain distinct phases of war-time service in the Methodist Protestant Church:

1. Our people gave generous financial support to the great cause. In every Liberty Loan Campaign and in every supplementary drive for the sale of War Savings Stamps, our Methodist Protestant leaders in every community served at the front in the home guard; and to the individual subscriptions of our people were superadded still larger purchases by our individual churches, our mission boards and our educational boards and institutions. Through direct representation on the American Commit-

tee for Armenian and Syrian Relief, now merged in the American Committee for Relief in the Near East, our Sunday-schools and churches made liberal contributions to the suffering Christians in the war zone. They contributed also with patriotic zeal and generosity to the Red Cross, the Young Men's Christian Association, the Young Women's Christian Association, and to every agency organized for the well-being of the soldiers. This responsive generosity has continued through the later calls of humanity in behalf of the hunger-stricken multitudes of the Near East and of China, and to every need that becomes an aftermath of the World War.

In this patriotic service our annual conferences and many of our distinct local agencies have supplemented in a very substantial way the work accomplished through the larger denominational channels.

2. The Methodist Protestant Church contributed, as we believe, her full proportionate share in ministering to the moral and religious life of the soldiers. Through the agency of our war-time commission and the Federal Council of the Churches of Christ in America, our denomination furnished her full quota of chaplains in the United States Army; and sent also a large number of her leaders to the service under the auspices of the Red Cross and the Red Triangle, together with a still larger number as religious work directors, camp pastors and public speakers in our American cantonments. The average record made by our representatives in these various fields has been so high as to gratify the just pride of our people, while the joy of service to the country and to the kingdom has been a true reward to these faithful soldiers of the flag and the cross.

While the spiritual leaders of our denomination were

performing their Christian duty in camp and field, our people have made in full measure the supreme sacrifice. Not our homes alone, but our pulpits and our colleges have sent their men into the Great War for the honor of America and for the freedom of the world, and the service flag in every church, in every Sunday-school, in every institution, tells the story of ready surrender to God and country.

3. The Methodist Protestant Church is seeking to do her share in the great work of reconstruction, and is organizing her various agencies for the purpose of widening the portals and strengthening the foundations of the home Church since the day when the boys came home; and is responsive to the challenge of humanity and the kingdom of God in behalf of the needy and groping millions over the sea. In this moral war work of the future, as in the military war work of the past, we are depending not alone upon the temporary agencies organized within our own bounds, but also upon the interdenominational channels so thoroughly mobilized by the Federal Council of the Churches of Christ in America.

The writer was Chairman of the war-time Commission of our denomination, and wishes to express the heartiest appreciation of the splendid service rendered by his associates in this work—Rev. Dr. Charles H. Beck and Rev. Dr. Charles E. Wilbur, both of whom were wise and loyal counselors in the consideration and solution of important questions in the midst of the great conflict.

It should be said also that, in addition to the patriotic service rendered by our Chaplains and by others hereinafter named, many of our denominational leaders laid down, for a time, their pastoral and educational duties to serve at once their country and their Lord, in the various forms of activity presented to them. Among these leaders were Rev. Dr. Thomas H. Lewis, Rev. Dr. Hugh Latimer Elderdice, Rev. Dr. John C. Broomfield, Rev. Dr. Fred A. Perry, Rev. Dr. Frank H. Lewis, Rev. Dr. Clarence L. Daugherty and many others.

CHAPLAINS IN COMMISSION

Rev. Harvey E. Orwick was born on a farm two miles east of Arlington, Ohio; and after graduating from the Westminster Theological Seminary, he entered the active ministry in the autumn of 1915, becoming a member of the Ohio Annual Conference. He was commissioned chaplain, with the military rank of first lieutenant, in the United States National Army, October 31, 1917, and was assigned to the 340th Infantry, 85th Division, but was transferred to the 7th Division in March, 1919.

Chaplain Orwick spent eighteen months in active service, and participated in the general offensive on the Meurthe-Moselle front, being in at the final roundup of the Great War November 9 to 11, 1918. Before going into the trenches and over the top in the final drive, his Division acted as reserves and supplies, functioning as a classification depot at the front.

Chaplain Orwick was the first Methodist Protestant minister to receive a chaplain's commission, and therefore, in point of service, becomes the ranking chaplain of our denomination; and he was one of the first sixty-five chaplains out of eleven hundred selected for service in the National Army. Chaplain Orwick fulfilled two distinct missions in the National Service; first of all, when his regiment was tented at Camp Custer, near Battle Creek, Michigan, and afterwards, to the end of the war, in the active fighting zone of the foreign service.   In both of these provinces he won the affectionate regard of the men and the unstinted praise of the officers in command.

The Infantry Regiments, on the later military model, were each supposed to have three chaplains, but Lieutenant Orwick was the only chaplain for the whole regiment, and in addition to his immediate religious functions he served as athletic, social and educational director of the regiment, and was thus brought into active co-operation with the Red Cross, the Young Men's Christian Association, the Salvation Army, and other kindred organizations.

Chaplain Orwick is now Professor of Physical Education in Adrian College, and the vigorous, healthful and happy Christianity which he puts into this new department greatly strengthens and enriches the atmosphere of the campus among the maples at Old Adrian.

Rev. Alden J. Green was born in Green Township, Randolph County, Indiana, and graduated from Adrian College in 1907. After serving one year, from September, 1907, to September, 1908, at Sully, Iowa, Brother Green was ordained by the North Illinois Conference in September, 1918, at Cuba, Illinois. Under appointment of this conference he was pastor at Bluffs, from September, 1908, to September, 1914; and at Cuba, Illinois, from September, 1914, to April, 1918; leaving his charge at this time in response to his appointment to chaplaincy by the United States government, he proceeded directly to Camp Zachary Taylor, near Louisville, Kentucky, and entered the Training School for Chaplains in April. He was commissioned chaplain, with the military rank of first lieutenant, May 29, 1918, and was ordered to report at General Headquarters in the American Expeditionary Forces for immediate assignment to duty.

Being assigned to duty with the 301st Stevedore Regiment, Chaplain Green was stationed with his military unit at St. Nazaire, France. This regiment was quartered in Camp No. 1, which was also classified as Camp Hospital No. 11, and containing barracks for the use of troops landing at St. Nazaire, and requiring a few days' rest before going forward. Chaplain Green here performed heroic service and nobly sought to realize the high ideals which led him across the sea in the service of his country. He preached almost every night to troops just landed, and accounts his ministry to men just arrived from home as one of the most pleasing memories of his career in the chaplaincy.

In September, 1918, Chaplain Green was transferred to the Second Division of the Regular Army, which was composed of the 9th and 23d Infantry Regiments; the 5th and 6th Regiments of Marines; the 12th, 15th, and 17th Field Artillery Regiments; the 2d Engineers, 2d Ammunition Train, 2d Supply Train and the 2d Sanitary Train. Two Field Hospital Units of the Sanitary Train were detailed to function as Hospital for Major Surgery, immediately back of the Infantry. Chaplain Green was assigned to duty in one of these Field Hospitals, and though it was possible occasionally to have a château for this humanitarian work, yet they were very often compelled to seek shelter under small tents which could be quickly put up or taken down. Chaplain Green and his men participated in various battles, including St. Mihiel, and the engagements connected with the Meuse-Argonne offensive, and finally he crossed the Rhine with the Army of Occupation, and performed his last public service in that important field.

Rev. Roy Irwin Farmer, having been recommended by the War-Time Commission of the Methodist Protestant Church, and having received the indorsement of the Committee on Army and Navy Chaplains of the Federal Council of Churches, received his appointment from the War Department October 4, 1918. He went directly to the Training School for Chaplains at Camp Taylor, Louisville, Kentucky. After the completion of his course, in which he made a fine record, he was commissioned first lieutenant and chaplain November 7, and was at once ordered to embark for over-seas service; but at this juncture, the armistice was signed and the order for his departure was of course countermanded, and he was sent instead to the Columbus barracks, Columbus, Ohio, for service under Colonel Johnson, commanding officer, and was discharged December 23, 1918.

Chaplain Farmer was born at Freeport, Ohio, October 25, 1888. After finishing the course of study in the public schools, he taught in Guernsey County for two years. Afterward, entering Adrian College, from which institution he graduated in 1916, with the degree of Bachelor of Arts, he then proceeded to the Yale Divinity School at New Haven, Connecticut, where he completed two years of work.

Upon his discharge from the army, Chaplain Farmer accepted the pastorate of the Second Methodist Protestant Church, Pittsburgh, Pennsylvania; but being a member of the Ohio Conference, he returned for work at the fall session and was assigned to the pastorate of the Conference Memorial Church at Zanesville, Ohio.

Rev. Roy Irwin Farmer has been equally successful in his student life at the college and the Divinity School, in the school for chaplains in preparation for war service, and in the large church which he has been called of the Lord to serve at Zanesville.

Rev. Perry E. Grimm, one of the honored chaplains representing the Methodist Protestant Church in the World War, was born in Ravenswood, West Virginia, November 30, 1888. His father was a farmer and remained on the farm until September, 1912.

Perry E. Grimm entered the Preparatory School at West Lafayette, Ohio, in September, 1912, and matriculated in West Lafayette College in September, 1914. September 16, 1916, he entered Adrian College, graduating from that institution in June, 1918.

While pastor of the St. Mary's charge, West Virginia Conference, to which he was appointed August 1, 1918, Mr. Grimm was recommended to the Federal Council for chaplaincy by the War Time Commission of the Methodist Protestant Church; was indorsed by the Committee of Army and Navy Chaplains of the Federal Council, and was duly appointed by the War Department, being sent to the Training School for Chaplains at Camp Taylor, Kentucky, from which he was graduated October 30, 1918.

He was immediately commissioned as first lieutenant and chaplain in the United States Army November 1, 1918, and served with the American Expeditionary Forces for a period of nine months. He was mustered out of service at Camp Dix, New Jersey, July 2, 1919.

Chaplain Grimm held student pastorates during his

college life, and since becoming a student in Westminster Theological Seminary, he has been very successful as a pastor in the fields of labor contiguous to Westminster; and he did loyal service during the last summer vacation at Stahlstown, within the bounds of the Pittsburgh Conference. And in this field of labor, as in his recent pastoral work in connection with his student life at Westminster, he has a most faithful and efficient co-worker in the person of his wife, Marie Beck Grimm, to whom he was married in September, 1919. He is now pastor of our First Church, Grafton, W. Va., and has before him a bright future in the ministry of the Methodist Protestant Church.

Rev. George G. Shurtz was born May 20, 1885, at West Lafayette, Ohio, and after his graduation from Adrian College and from the Westminster Theological Seminary, entered the ministry of the Methodist Protestant Church in the Muskingum Conference, now the Ohio. The beginning of the war found him in the midst of a splendid career as pastor of the Muskingum Conference Memorial Church at Zanesville, Ohio. He was commissioned chaplain, with the military rank of first lieutenant, March 3, 1918, and immediately went to Camp Sherman, and was soon assigned to the 308th Regiment of Engineers. He left with his regiment for Camp Merritt, May 24, 1918, and sailed for Europe, June 3, on the British transport, *Khyber*. Chaplain Shurtz and his men were thirteen days in crossing the Atlantic, being protected in transit by British battleships, and landed in Liverpool June 16, 1918. From Liverpool he went to Southampton and sailed from there to La Havre, landing in France June 19, 1918. After a few days in camp, Chaplain Shurtz and his regiment were sent forward to Rimacourt in France to prepare for actual service.

The record of Chaplain Shurtz in the Great War was honorable in the highest degree, and won at once the affectionate regard of the soldier boys, and compelled the recognition of the officers of every rank. A number of his descriptive letters appeared in the "Methodist Recorder," and one of his reports to the president of the General Conference, throwing noonday light upon certain moral issues in the army, was forwarded to the National War-Time Commission of the Churches, and the helpful suggestions embodied in his report won attention and recognition at American Headquarters across the sea.

Returning from the war Rev. George G. Shurtz found many doors of opportunity opened wide to him and received calls from leading churches in different conferences, but finally accepted the pastorate of our historic church at Tiffin, Ohio, where he is now engaged with his loyal people in the building of a splendid new house of worship.

Rev. Montgomery J. Shroyer, who is now a professor in Westminster Theological Seminary, was born at Yorktown, Indiana, and entered the ministry in August, 1915, and was ordained by the Indiana Conference, August 21, 1916. He was commissioned chaplain, with the military rank of first lieutenant, November 7, 1918, and soon after that date was assigned to the important military unit known as the United States General Hospital No. 24, located at Parkview Station, Pittsburgh, Pennsylvania. After a service of eight and one-half months he was discharged July 28, 1919.

In his appointment to the highly important work at Parkview, Chaplain Shroyer was designated the Morale Officer; and his work among the men was a helpful and noble ministry from first to last. He was the only chaplain in the institution; and his impartial concern for the welfare of the soldier boys of every creed, together with his wise and sympathetic approach to the men who had wandered away from their God, won the hearty approval and enthusiastic support of everybody in the whole environment, including both officers and men. And so it came to pass, in recognition of his true merit in this responsible position he was promoted to a captaincy, May 8, 1919.

The periodical published by the soldiers at Parkview was christened by Chaplain Shroyer himself and he gave it the unique and appropriate name, "Asyouwere"; and the columns of this spirited and brilliant little paper were greatly enriched by the gifted pen of Chaplain Shroyer.

Rev. J. R. Wright, of the Maryland Conference, enlisted as a chaplain in the United States Army in August, 1917, and served eighteen months in France, and on his return to the United States became Division Chaplain at Camp Pike, Arkansas.

Chaplain Wright was born in Cumberland, Maryland, December 25, 1884, and united with the First Methodist Protestant Church of that city on probation, February 17, 1901, being elected to full membership December 15 of the same year. He joined the Maryland Conference as an itinerant in 1909 and was ordained in 1911.

While a student at the Westminster Theological Seminary, he served Williamsport charge, now called Harmony. In 1909 he was pastor at Campbell, and from 1909 to 1912 at Amelia; from 1913 to 1914 at Queen Anne's, and 1915, 1916 and 1917 at Mount Tabor.

Chaplain Wright was an earnest and faithful pastor and an able minister of the Word; and he made a splendid record throughout his whole career as a chaplain of the United States Army.

Rev. Coral D. Payne was born near Spencer, Roane County, West Virginia, November 20, 1893. He was graduated from the Westminster Theological Seminary, in May, 1917, and was soon afterwards appointed by the president of the West Virginia Conference as a supply to the Methodist Protestant Church, at Point Marion, Pennsylvania. He was ordained to the ministry in the West Virginia Conference, at Morgantown, August 26, 1917, and was returned to Point Marion as his first regular charge.

Having volunteered his services for a chaplaincy in the United States Army, he was duly appointed and received orders to report August 23, 1918, to the Training School for Chaplains, at Camp Taylor, Louisville, Kentucky. He was commissioned chaplain, with the military rank of first lieutenant, September 26, 1918, and on the same date received orders from Washington to report to the Commanding General of the American Expeditionary Forces. From October 24 to November 20, 1918, he served with the 101st Infantry of the 26th Division, and from the latter date to July 16, 1919, he was connected with the Field Hospital section of the 7th Army Corps of the 3d Army.

Chaplain Payne was discharged from the service July 16, 1919, and at the West Virginia Conference in the early fall of the same year he was appointed to our important church at Grafton, W. Va.; and has now become pastor of the Squirrel Hill Church, Pittsburgh, Pa. His work thus far has been very successful, and he is giving to the army of the Lord the same faithful, efficient and valiant service which he gave to his country and to humanity in the Great War. His father, Rev. Josiah Payne, is one of the leading ministers of the West Virginia Conference.

F. W. Perkins, D.D., was recommended for a chaplaincy by the Federal Council early in 1918, and, having been indorsed by the War Department, was duly accepted and entered the School for Chaplains at Camp Taylor, Kentucky, graduating from that institution July 3, 1918, and receiving his commission October 16, 1918, as first lieutenant and chaplain, and was immediately assigned to the Tank Corps and went into camp near Gettysburg; but the signing of the armistice and the close of the war occurred only a few days after his arrival there, and he soon returned to his pastoral work at New Brighton, Pennsylvania.

Rev. Archibald R. Corn, one of the chaplains representing the Methodist Protestant Church in the World War, was born in Washington County, Kentucky, and was ordained to the ministry August, 1912, becoming a member of the Indiana Conference. After serving as pastor of the Avalon Park Methodist Protestant Church, Chicago, he was pastor of several important charges in Indiana Conference, including Bryant, Liberty Center,

Hanfield, and the Villa Avenue Church, Indianapolis.

He received his commission as first lieutenant and chaplain at the Training School for Chaplains, Camp Taylor, Kentucky, September 26, 1918. On the same day he was ordered to France, but was granted a few days in which to arrange business matters and to visit relatives. On the fifteenth day of October he sailed on the transport *Agamemnon* and landed at Brest, October 26. On his arrival in France he was sent to Le Mons and Le Chateau d'Aux in connection with the Chaplains' School. He was assigned to the 312th Infantry of the 78th Division, on the Meuse-Argonne front. Chaplain Corn was with his regiment in the rest camp of the Argonne forest when the armistice was signed; but on November 11, at 11 A.M. they marched through St. Menehould to La Ville Dampierre.

He thought this a very appropriate time to have a Thanksgiving service, and accordingly very impressive services were held on Thursday night of that week. After a week in that village he moved south to Semur, which became the Divisional Headquarters until May, 1919, at which time the Division returned home.

Rev. W. L. Hamrick was born at Schamberville, Mississippi, March 13, 1886, and entered the ministry in the Mississippi Conference of the Methodist Protestant Church, March, 1906, before he had reached his twentieth birthday. He was commissioned chaplain, with the military rank of first lieutenant April 15, 1918, and was ordered to report to Kelly Field for immediate duty. He was assigned to the Second Training Brigade, Air Service, in which unit he served until July of the same year, when a re-organization of the field led to his permanent assignment to Kelly Field No. 2, which was the flying field proper. He continued in the service at this place until his discharge, nine months after receiving his commission.

Of the eight chaplains comprising the personnel of the religious service at Kelly Field, Chaplain Hamrick was the fourth to arrive and the first to conduct devotional services in the Field Hospital, and was also the first to hold a united service for the entire Brigade. This larger meeting was held on Mother's Day, and was made notable by the filling of several mail pouches with letters to the mothers of the soldier boys. This unique service was participated in by the commanding officer and was highly commended by him.

Chaplain Hamrick worked among the soldiers with great zeal and consecration during the influenza epidemic. In recognition of his merit he was recommended by his Field Executive officer for promotion to a captaincy a few weeks before his discharge; and the consummation of this honor was only prevented by the close of the war. Chaplain Hamrick, in common with all the Christian patriots who failed to reach the war zone, was keenly disappointed because of his inability to serve at the front, but he was very popular at Kelly Field, and officers and soldiers alike paid tribute to his fidelity and efficiency.

Brother Hamrick is one of the progressive young ministers of the Texas Conference, a representative in the General Conference, and is the popular and successful pastor of our church at Cooper.

Rev. Ivan J. Howland, now president of the Onondaga Conference, received his appointment as religious director at Camp Dix, under the auspices of the Young Men's

Christian Association; but his pastoral obligations were so great, as urged by the quarterly conference of the charge he was then serving, that he finally concluded to remain with the Church.

Rev. S. F. Sliker, of the Eastern Conference, enlisted in the service under the auspices of the Young Men's Christian Association, and after a course of preparation at Springfield College, Springfield, Massachusetts, became physical director at Camp Stewart, Virginia. He remained in that position until May 1, 1919, when, on his own request, he was relieved from duty as camp director and became hut director, thus returning to the work in which he had already spent two months prior to his becoming camp director. September 15, 1919, he was sent to Camp Eustis, Virginia, where he became religious director, and where he remained until October 9, when he resigned to take up work as pastor in the Eastern Conference.

Rev. A. T. Rebey, of the Fort Smith-Oklahoma Conference, performed faithful and efficient work as camp pastor.

Rev. J. S. Eddins, now pastor of the Bibb Street Church, Montgomery, Alabama, served as camp pastor at Camp Sheridan, in the city of Montgomery, looking up the names of all Methodist Protestants in the camp, and rendering valuable service in many ways to the soldier boys. Many of the young men attended his church services. Brother Eddins is now president of the Young People's Union of the Alabama Conference.

Rev. R. C. Stubbins, of the North Carolina Conference, after passing through the officers' training course at Blue Ridge, North Carolina, under the auspices of the Young Men's Christian Association, was appointed religious secretary at Camp Wheeler, Macon, Georgia. After serving there for one month, Rev. R. C. Stubbins was called home by the sudden and serious illness of his wife, and remained thereafter in pastoral work, becoming minister of the First Methodist Protestant Church at Greensboro, North Carolina.

Rev. William H. Litsinger gave four months to religious work in the United States Army, this period of service extending from May 1 to August 31, 1918. He entered this service as a representative of the North Baltimore Church, which granted him leave of absence from pastoral duties "for such time and such place" as he might arrange with the Young Men's Christian Association. His regular salary was continued by his loyal people throughout the whole period of his connection with the Army, and he therefore accepted only his actual expenses from the funds of the "Y."

Rev. Mr. Litsinger's first appointment was at Camp Holabird, where he spent a month organizing the "Y" work. Desiring, however, to do more definite religious work, he accepted an invitation to Camp Meade as Religious Work Secretary; and in the latter half of his sojourn at this camp he served as Religious Work Director. It fell to the lot of Rev. Mr. Litsinger to serve chiefly with newly enlisted men, and in this connection he was enabled to exert a most salutary influence upon the men in khaki. While he exercised the duties of Hut Secretary he was in the Depot Brigade. During a single week in the later period of his service there were four hundred Christian confessions reported from the fourteen stations of the camp. This report is in itself a silent but eloquent tribute to the good work performed by Rev. Mr. Litsinger.

Rev. J. L. Nichols, of the Maryland Conference, signed up with the Young Men's Christian Association in February, 1919, and entered upon the duties of Hut Secretary for overseas service. He sailed from New York March 14, 1918, landing at Bordeaux on the 24th. On the 25th of the same month, being about the third day of the bombardment of Paris with a long-range gun, he landed in the French capital and remained there one week for special lectures and preparation for the service upon which he was about to enter. Early in April he was detailed to start a Young Men's Christian Association unit in Aviation Acceptance Park No. 1, the location of this hut being only five miles from Paris on the Road D'Italie, otherwise called the Fontainebleau Road. In a few months the work became too large for the tent in which the work was started and a double Adrian barrack hut was therefore erected, Rev. Mr. Nichols having general management of this work, with from six to eight Young Men's Christian Association assistants, and from ten to twelve soldiers to form the personnel of this very efficient center of influence.

In October of the same year, not being able to throw off the aftermath of the influenza which had attacked him in August, and feeling the necessity of a change for his health, he asked to be transferred to the front-line trenches. This courageous request was granted and Mr. Nichols was sent to the Toul sector, with the army which was advancing toward Metz. Here for awhile he had charge of the religious work of the whole Division. The armistice was signed very soon after this, and he then took charge of the main hut at Pont à Mousson, only twenty miles from Metz; and here Rev. Mr. Nichols served the boys as they came out of the trenches. He remained until the middle of February, 1919, when he asked to be re-assigned to religious work, that he might engage in an evangelistic campaign under Dr. King, of Oberlin College, who had general supervision of that work. In this truly ministerial work he remained for some time, visiting camps and billets and holding meetings with the men until March, when, his year having expired, and the war being over, he returned to America, leaving Brest on the 4th of March, 1919, and reaching New York, March 13, 1919, but still working as transport secretary aboard ship as he crossed the Atlantic.

Rev. Jesse L. Buckley, who is now pastor of the Victory Memorial Methodist Protestant Church, Indianapolis, Indiana, organized the first unit of the Red Cross at Port William, Ohio; and this step so increased the interest in the movement as to lead to the organization of a strong chapter also at Wilmington, Ohio. He volunteered his services to the Young Men's Christian Association for overseas work; but his success as an organizer led to his being retained in America. After a sojourn in Atlantic City, where he received preparatory instructions, he was put in charge of Clinton County and requested to raise $10,000 for overseas work. He organized the county so thoroughly, and followed up the organization so strenuously with his own personal effort that he went over the top, securing $13,000. Rev. Mr.

Buckley was then asked to organize the county for the Third Liberty Loan, and to act as field secretary in the good cause. Many had thought it impossible to secure the sum allotted to that county; but after Brother Buckley had thoroughly prepared the way, a great drive was instituted and the county met its quota in full.

After another successful drive in the interest of the Red Cross work, and after splendid achievements also in connection with the food conservation program, he was given a still broader mission in connection with the Council of National Defense, being made county executive secretary. After this promotion he moved to Wilmington, where the Commercial Club furnished splendid office facilities for this important work, and where Mr. Buckley won distinction by his notable success in this patriotic service. He continued this work until called to his present field in Indianapolis.

XIX

THE LOGIC OF CHURCH UNION

THE various steps in the process by which the Methodist Protestant Church and the Church of the United Brethren in Christ finally reached a basis of union is familiar to the readers of our own denomination. But the decisive events and the final issue of the movement deserve a brief review and a permanent record; and the author of this book, having been President of the General Conference throughout the period covering these negotiations, desires to make plain, once for all, the mandatory nature of the authority upon which the negotiations were begun, the unquestioned fairness of the mutual agreement finally reached, and the clearness of the decision recorded in favor of the proposed union by the voting units of both denominations.

The Methodist Protestant Church had already indulged in experimental negotiations with a number of kindred churches; and the result, in almost every case, was disappointing in the highest degree. While the Methodist Protestants of the North and South were temporarily separated by the issues of the Civil War, the southern branch of our own church and the Methodist Episcopal Church, South, united in a mutual approach toward a basis of union; but, the moment fixed conditions emerged from the realm of sentiment, a practical agreement was found impossible. And the one unfortunate sequel to this movement was the disruption of the Virginia Conference of the Methodist Protestant Church, while certain influences set in motion by this movement, and encouraged by other causes, resulted in serious losses to several of our Southern conferences.

During the same period of separation, the Methodist Protestant Church of the North, then called simply the Methodist Church, had a kindred experience with the Wesleyan Methodist Church. In this case a very satisfactory basis of union was adopted, and a joint session for the final merging of the two denominations was appointed to be held in Cleveland, Ohio. But while the Methodist Protestants were there in full representative numbers, only three or four of the Wesleyan Methodists made their appearance, and the majority of their churches ultimately renounced the union and held fast to their original name.

One of the most promising movements in the direction of church union was that which brought the Congregationalists, the Methodist Protestants and the United Brethren into serious negotiations, and almost to the point of union. But even this mutual approach of kindred churches was finally halted and defeated by mere incidents rather than by real obstacles; and that movement, because it led to mutual acquaintance and sympathy between our own Church and the United Brethren, essentially linked the one series of negotiations with the other. The decision to enter upon negotiations with the United Brethren Church was reached by the unanimous action of our own General Conference at Baltimore, in 1912, this action being taken, however, in response to fraternal addresses by Rev. Dr. W. H. Washinger and Rev. A. P. Funkhouser, of the United Brethren Church. This enactment was embodied in the following resolution offered by Rev. Dr. F. T. Tagg:

"We believe that a union of the Methodist Protestant Church and the Church of the United Brethren in Christ is both practical and desirable, and we therefore authorize our commission on church union to enter into negotiations with the commission of the Church of the United Brethren in Christ, just as soon as that commission is fully authorized to enter upon such negotiations."

The following supplementary resolution, offered by Rev. Dr. George H. Miller and Rev. Dr. Crates S. Johnson, was also adopted unanimously:

"Resolved, That if in their negotiations for union with the Church of the United Brethren in Christ, the Methodist Episcopal Church, or the Methodist Episcopal Church, South, our commission on church union should find speedy action advisable, they are hereby authorized to overture the annual conferences in regard thereto, and, upon favorable action of two-thirds of the annual conferences, they shall call a special session of this General Conference, in accordance with constitutional provisions, to act thereon."

In simple obedience to the instructions given us in these resolutions, we entered into joint session with the representatives of the Church of the United Brethren in Christ, and a Basis of Union was the final result of our negotiations.

The Basis of Union, which was a constitutional agreement, covering and safeguarding the fundamental principles of the two denominations, was adopted unanimously by the joint commissioners at the last Columbus meeting, was indorsed by more than the required two-thirds of our annual conferences, and by more than the required three-fourths of the United Brethren annual conferences, and also by the two General Conferences.

The Basis of Union reaffirmed and safeguarded those great principles which are identical in the two denominations; those principles which are cherished equally by every member of the Methodist Protestant Church and every member of the United Brethren Church; those principles which, flowing with equal flood in the hearts of these two peoples, first suggested, as by the mutual impulse of liberty, the possibility of this proposed union. What were these principles? The mutual rights of ministers and laymen! The right of appeal, to be maintained inviolate forever! The right of private judgment in the field of interpretation! The recognition of but one order in the ministry, all elders of the Church of God being equal! These were every one recognized and safeguarded in this Basis of Union.

The progress of the union movement was doubtless hindered, and perhaps the consummation of the union was finally prevented, by a number of reactionary influences.

The first of these was a reversal of the promised campaign of education. Certain agencies which were officially committed to the movement by the authoritative action of the two churches, and which were even directed to launch a campaign favorable to the union, lent themselves to the opposition. These reactionary influences were busy indeed in both denominations, and in such equal proportions that the malcontents of the one church could readily find an excuse, if not a reason, for their own opposition by calling attention to some adverse action or adverse propaganda in the other church.

But the unbroken line of procedure in the Methodist Protestant Church soon carried the cause beyond the reach of the opposition; and agitation on the union question happily ceased in the Methodist Protestant Church, with the conclusive action at Columbus, and I invited the attention of our annual conferences at their very next session, both through addresses and suggestive resolutions, to the progressive development of our own denomination. The status of the subject, in its relation to our own work, found expression in my quadrennial address to the General Conference at Zanesville, in this way:

"And although we have entered into certain negotiations for church union, in explicit obedience to the command of the General Conference, and even into certain agreements, we have constantly made plain to all the Christian world, and must forever continue to make plain, that we will never surrender any of the larger units of value in our ecclesiastical manor; that we will never part with the seed-principles of our polity; that we will especially guard and cherish those family jewels which are known in the sacred archives of our history as the mutual rights of the ministry and the laity.

"Our own duty at this important moment is therefore very plain. Having recorded our covenant-mutual, having completed the circuit of our own procedure, having driven our stakes at the corners, and fixed the bounds of our agreements to the line and to the plummet, there is nothing more in the field of church union to engage our immediate attention or to worry our hearts. I have all confidence in the sincerity of those who have negotiated with us, and I appreciate, with comprehending sympathy, the obstacles that lie in the converging paths of church union; paths which are for the most part still unopened, and the course of which leads through uncharted regions.

"But I thank God with a glad heart to-day that our denominational record on this subject is such that we stand before the Christian world in an attitude of equal independence and honor; and, whether the union is finally consummated or finally unrealized, our present duty, here and now, is that of devoting ourselves, a living sacrifice, to the progressive future of the Methodist Protestant Church."

In the United Brethren Church, however, the postponement of the referendum gave opportunity to the opposition; and, while the engineers were presumably off guard, somebody mounted the train, reversed the engine, and ran it backward for two full years; and, at the end of the journey, tacitly exclaimed: "Just see where we are! We can never reach the union junction!"

But the reversal of the records is even more lamentable than the reversal of the campaign of education. The psychology of delay in itself would have been almost fatal; and the inertia of a halted movement in the progress of the Kingdom is harder to overcome than the active opposition of the whole world. That explains why the Allegheny Conference of the United Brethren Church could be classified as against the union in 1919 at Wichita notwithstanding the recorded fact that the same conference, ministers and lay delegates voting together in equal numbers, declared for the union in 1913 by a vote of one hundred and thirty-eight to two. In a word the question is not as to how any particular conference would vote now, but rather as to how that conference would have voted at the time when the logical procedure of the movement, and the universal expectation of the laity, called for the plebiscite. But more serious still is the fact that a long delay permits even the best-informed leaders to forget the official record of the union vote in the two churches. For example, it was stated on the floor of the United Brethren General Conference at Wichita that the North Carolina Conference of the Methodist Protestant Church had voted overwhelmingly against the union notwithstanding the fact that North Carolina had voted for the union more than two to one—fifty-five to twenty-three; and a like misunderstanding of our recorded vote was disclosed in the same discussion as to other annual conferences. And kindred misunderstandings perhaps were sown broadcast among our own people, as to events and conditions in the United Brethren Church.

But the failure of the Board of Bishops to take the vote of the United Brethren people will forever remain an unforgotten mystery to every Methodist Protestant in America. For, as we understand the matter, the General Conference at Decatur did not empower the bishops to decide as to whether the plebiscite should be taken or not taken, but only as to the particular date of the referendum, within a reasonable time after the next prior step in the procedure; the same authority, indeed, and the same limitations, which govern the annual conference presidents of our Methodist Protestant Church in fixing a specific date for a duly-called special session of our own General Conference.

Nothwithstanding this long delay and because I still felt the burden of responsibility in common with my fellow-commissioners I sought to open a wider door of agreement in my address before the General Conference of the United Brethren Church at Wichita, speaking on this phase of the subject as follows:

"I desire to suggest broader negotiations; or rather to focus attention upon a plan already proposed in former negotiations; a plan by which we may finally conserve all that we have gained and yet merge the current of our union movement with all the meeting streams of the Christian world. I find the suggestion and the prophecy of this larger program in our Indianapolis agreement, an instrument which closed with an invitation to all denominations of "like faith and polity" to join with us, on the broad and simple basis of union adopted at Columbus. With that enlarged agreement as a starting-point, may we not go forth on the highways of a new hope, and humbly sound the trumpet-call for the progressive federation and the final union of the whole Republican hemisphere of American Christianity? With such ideals before us, what glorious things we may achieve for God and humanity, as kindred democracies in the Christian world!"

While negotiations were still pending however between the Methodist Protestant Church and the Church of the United Brethren in Christ, the General Conference of the Methodist Episcopal Church met at Saratoga Springs, New York; and inasmuch as our own General Conference had at its last session appointed me fraternal messenger to that body, I accordingly attended the Saratoga meeting. And because unofficial counter-movements were abroad in the field of church union presumably growing out of a misunderstanding as to the real situation I undertook to make plain to the leaders of the Methodist Episcopal Church that we were still honor-bound to the United Brethren. The following paragraphs cover what I was led to say on this subject:

"The progressive affiliation of kindred Churches has also revealed those natural affinities of history, of doctrine and of polity which point the way to still closer fellowship, and, if possible, to final union. Obviously, such a process will often point the way to a union of like with like, rather than a union of name with name. For the content of a name changes very often with the passing of the years, while likeness answers to itself, always, from day to day, in every epoch. It naturally suggests itself, therefore, that every step toward affiliation or union would be found mutually shorter on the one hand between kindred democracies among the Churches, and between those, on the other hand, which are alike Episcopal in form of government. And the final consummation of a united Protestant Christianity will be hastened also, as I believe, by first grouping the smaller denominations, both because they can approach one another on comparatively equal terms, and because being once united they are then prepared to meet the larger denominations on somewhat equal terms.

"In harmony with this natural process our own Methodist Protestant Church entered into negotiations with the Church of the United Brethren in Christ, these negotiations resulting two years ago in a basis of union. The two General Conferences, as well as the required number of the Annual Conferences of both denominations, have adopted this basis of union and the only step which remains to be taken is that of the referendum vote by the United Brethren people.

"These two churches are, of course, officially honorbound to this movement until it is officially terminated. The basis of union adopted is simple, broad, and fundamental; following closely the lines of the tri-Church syllabus of an earlier date. And as the last deliverance of the joint commission closed with an invitation to other Churches of like doctrine and polity to join us in this movement, it is hoped that delay in the consummation of this proposed union may widen its scope and include other kindred Churches.

"The progressive affiliation of kindred Churches has revealed the fact that the highest union, in the purpose of God, may sometimes take the form of a reciprocal interdependence rather than that of organic union. The united movements of kindred Churches are brought about, not by the mutual sacrifice of cherished principles, but by the mutual interchange of cherished principles; not by mutual surrender but by mutual appropriation. For the distinctive features of the great denominations, as I believe, are not opposites one to another in the philosophy of the Kingdom, but rather complements one to the other; and in the long afterward of the providence of God they will prove to have been points of contact and of union.

"And so let us humbly believe that God may have sometimes intervened to prevent a contemplated organic union, for the sake of that more substantial union, which, through complementary forces, He is Himself working out to the final sum of things; and that, therefore, He may often intend us simply to live closer together, simply to have each other, just as we are; being good denominational neighbors and learning above all in ecclesiastical life as well as in our personal relations to love our neighbors as ourselves!"

The next succeeding General Conference of the Methodist Protestant Church, meeting at Zanesville, Ohio, had the pleasure of receiving Bishop G. M. Matthews, D.D., and Rev. R. K. Funk, D.D., as fraternal messengers from the Church of the United Brethren in Christ; and the writer, as General Conference President, in company with Rev. Dr. Chas. H. Beck, our General Conference Secretary, visited the United Brethren General Conference at Wichita, and mutual love abounded from first to last between the representatives of the two negotiating churches.

But inasmuch as the referendum vote of the United Brethren people was still postponed, with no decisive action concerning this important and essential procedure, and, finding that my own judgment was in harmony with

that of our own Commissioners, I published the following message to the Methodist Protestant Church:

"In the firm belief that the time has come for a conclusive declaration as to the status of church union in
the Methodist Protestant Church, with the keenest remembrance of our happy associations with the splendid
Christian gentlemen of the United Brethren Church, and
with fraternal and loving benedictions upon every member of that great communion we give our official opinion
as follows:

"1. The failure of the bishops of the United Brethren
Church to specify a definite time for the referendum
vote ordered by their General Conference, becomes a
de facto withdrawal from the agreement officially made
with our denomination; and therefore all negotiations for
union between the Methodist Protestant Church and the
Church of the United Brethren in Christ are fully and
finally terminated.

"2. The question of union as an open proposition between our own church and other denominations was
merged in the specific basis of union with the Church of
the United Brethren in Christ, the general commission
appointed at Baltimore being officially superseded by the
special commission appointed at Columbus; and therefore, with the discontinuance of negotiations with the
United Brethren, the union question, in its every relation,
disappears from our current denominational program,
and no further negotiations with any denomination can
be legally initiated, unless they are begun, *de novo,* by
the future action of the General Conference.

"And I will venture one further opinion, an opinion
which, though it is personal and not official, is inspired
by jealous anxiety for the undying principle of mutual
rights bequeathed to us by the fathers. I venture the
declaration that the Methodist Protestant Church, having voyaged fifteen years and more on the restless sea
of union movements and counter-movements, has discharged her full duty in that direction and has earned

the right to sail a straightforward course, manning her own ship and flying her own flag."

This opinion was manifestly in harmony with the judgment of the General Conference at Greensboro; for when a communication came up from one of the conferences favoring Methodist Protestant coöperation with the movement for Methodist union on episcopal lines, it was negatived unanimously through indefinite postponement both by the committee on Coöperative Christianity and by the General Conference itself. It still remains true that we now have no standing Commission on church union; and it still remains true that the union question cannot be revived in the Methodist Protestant Church unless it arises *de novo* from the people themselves, or from their chosen representatives in General Conference assembled.

XX

THE CHALLENGE OF TO-MORROW

THE General Conference of 1916 launched a series of progressive movements for the quadrennium, and these movements had their prophetic beginnings at once in the initial action of a number of our Annual Conferences and in the spontaneous promptings of the people. The Great War was already at high tide in the Old World, with foreshadowings of American fellowship of sacrifice with the champions of freedom and civilization over the high seas. And already the war had opened wide the door to new and unfamiliar problems in Church and State alike; and every wide-awake Christian in all the earth felt, more keenly than ever before, the weight of a world-wide responsibility. New ideals were abroad among the churches of Christ in America, and our own denomination felt the thrill of the new era.

The members of the General Conference, assembled at Zanesville, Ohio, in 1916, were truly representative of the Methodist Protestant Church in its most progressive mood and were truly responsive to the great problems which were knocking at the gates of the Kingdom.

In the judgment of the General Conference, and in the judgment of those who in various Annual Conferences had already initiated onward movements in their own local fields, two great hemispheres of ecclesiastical life loomed largest of all. Christian Missions and Christian Education filled the horizon everywhere, and every man who had caught the vision of the hour desired to strengthen the boards and institutions of the Church, with special reference to the Christianizing of America through deeper and broader interest in the cause of Home Missions; to the sending of the gospel abroad to the very ends of the earth; and to the planting on firmer foundations of Christian schools of higher education in our own country.

To accomplish these ends, the General Conference of 1916 launched a great forward movement, having a manifold purpose, and looking to the symmetrical development of the Church in every zone of activity. In the one realm this movement proposed a 25 per cent gain in the membership during the four years; one candidate for the ministry to every five hundred members; one college student to every two hundred members, with a campaign of evangelism for the realization of these ideals. In the financial hemisphere the movement proposed a million dollar campaign for our boards and institutions.

For the realization of these and kindred objects embodied in the program of the movement, the president of the General Conference was authorized and directed to appoint a Forward Movement Commission. To this important commission I appointed Rev. John C. Broomfield, D.D., of Fairmont, W. Va.; Rev. Charles D. Sinkinson, D.D., of Atlantic City, N. J.; Rev. J. M. Gill, D.D., of Baltimore, Md.; Rev. W. W. Lineberry, D.D., of Jonesboro, Ind.; Hon. J. F. Cappel, of Uhrichsville, Ohio; Mr. Levi Custis, of Sabina, Ohio, and Mr. Frank Ewing, of Pittsburgh, Pa.

The General Conference elected Rev. Crates S. Johnson, D.D., of Columbus, Ohio, as the Executive Secretary of the Forward Movement Commission. Dr. Johnson was born in Indiana and entered the ministry of the Methodist Protestant Church in the capital city of that state, and rounded out his splendid career in the pastoral office at Tiffin, Ohio, and at the First Church, Columbus, giving evidence of his genius for conducting a financial campaign by the successful raising of a large fund for the Superannuated Preachers' Aid Society of the Muskingum Conference. As soon as he was released from the pastorate of the First Church, Columbus, Dr. Johnson entered at once upon the duties of the denominational office to which he had been elected; and at the high tide of the forward movement, and in preparation for the financial drive for the million dollars, he removed to Pittsburgh that he might be more closely associated with his fellow workers in the good cause.

In the meantime I felt called upon, as General Conference president, to differentiate "the one million dollars for our boards and institutions" from the regular annual budget and annual conference interests.

The Executive Committee, in their meeting at Indianapolis, had voted to credit the annual budget as a part of the mandatory million; but this action was not put forward as an interpretation of the action of the General Conference, but merely expressed the judgment of the committee as to the responsive ability and willingness of the Church. But it soon became manifest that no clear-cut and appealing challenge could be made to the Church while the annual budget was subject to annual change, and while the sums realized from the budget were so variable. And besides minor considerations such as this, a great whirlwind of war had swept over the earth, beating humanity into the dust; and all the world was crying for light and love; and every one of our colleges, as well as our seminary and our mission fields, needed, each for itself, the whole of the million dollars. And so I presumed to release the goal from all confusion with the budget and to press the General Conference claim in all its integrity, lifting the cry, "One million for the Master."

And then came the instant and loyal response of the Executive Committee, and the hearty indorsement of the Big Four of the Forward Movement Commission, Dr. Broomfield, Dr. Dinkinson, Dr. Gill and Dr. Lineberry, and our five great secretaries, Dr. Klein, with all the Orient in his great heart; and Dr. Beck, with the well-trained vision which sees at once the door of opportunity and the key that unlocks it; and Dr. Johnson, with a genius for bringing facts and figures to the fore and visualizing them to the eye of the Church; and Dr. Miller, who knows how to throw the Lord's net into the deepest waters, and to bring forth sure results for the Kingdom; and Dr. Dixon, with his flaming enthusiasm for the work of the young people and the upbuilding of the Kingdom; and, last but not least, that splendid galaxy of leaders known as the Campaign Central Committee.

The Campaign Central Committee was so essentially important to the financial consummation of the Forward Movement that we pause here for a word of appreciation. The Campaign Central Committee comprised the Forward Movement Commission as a whole, the president and the executive secretary of each of the several boards and institutions, the presidents of our educational institutions and the editors of the Church papers, with the president of the General Conference as ex-officio chairman, and the secretary of the General Conference as ex-officio secretary. This commission, functioning as it did through the various zone committees, with a progressive leader in every Annual Conference to champion the movement throughout his own district, developed a high degree of efficiency and was enabled to reach the last church, if not the last individual unit, in our denominational territory.

What was the result of the Forward Movement? We did not realize indeed "One Million for the Master," but we succeeded in raising more money for our boards and institutions than they had received through denominational budgets and annual offerings for the whole twenty years preceding this wide-awake quadrennium. It was a worthy achievement for any church to have made so great a departure from its habitual paths in the field of Christian benevolences; and, moreover, the six hundred thousand dollars actually received came as a special providence to many of our institutions and to our missionary fields both at home and abroad. And the happiest record of all is that which discloses the spiritual awakening which accompanied the financial drive of the million dollar campaign. The Methodist Protestant Church, in common with all the churches of Christ in America of almost every creed, suffered a sharp reaction in church attendance and a loss in aggregate membership, but our losses were not greater than those of other communions; and over against our war-time losses we made a net gain of seven thousand members during the same period in which we were realizing so largely our financial objectives.

A misunderstanding has gone abroad as to the alleged membership loss in our denomination during the quadrennium covering the Great War. This mistake arose from the fact that the reports for the Muskingum Conference were not included in the numbers from which comparison was made, this clerical inadvertence arising from a confusion of the Greater Ohio Conference reports with the reports of the two separate conferences.

The gain of seven thousand in membership in the year 1919 is equivalent to an increase of almost four per cent, and this represents a rebound as immediate and an increase as great as was experienced by any other denomination in America.

But, forgetting the things which are behind, and stretching to the things which lie on before, the Methodist Protestant Church must face the challenge of the future.

Coleridge has said that "in to-day already walks to-morrow"; and this is peculiarly true of the prophetic movements of the kingdom of God. Yesterday was the seedsower; to-day is the reaper. To-day is the seedsower; to-morrow will be the reaper. The best preparation for the work of the future is to be gained, not by empty visions of coming achievement, not by lifting up our eyes afar to the dreamlands of idle expectation, but by steadfast devotion to the everyday tasks that await us in the broad field of duty.

One of the needs of the hour is that of denominational loyalty; not sectarian loyalty, not loyalty for the sake of the denomination itself alone, but loyalty to whatever denominational principles and ideals are true enough and big enough to form a genuine complement in the sum of Christian truth.

What is denominational loyalty? Instead of a definition, let us turn to a true analogy. Denominational loyalty occupies the same place in the religious world that patriotism occupies in the political world. Many a political leader condemns, in the most vigorous terms, what he is pleased to call sectarianism, forgetful of the fact that, in the true analogy of these two hemispheres of life, loyalty to one's church is on the same high level as loyalty to one's country, and treason to one's church is on the same low level as treason to one's country. What is civilization itself but a composite of national traits and characteristics? And the man who contributes most to civilization is the man who does most and best for the development of those distinctive forces of civilization for which his own country stands. Great Britain's contribution to human progress was made by the development of whatever civilizing forces were exceptionally British; and the evolution of these forces went on for a thousand years, emerging from conflicts innumerable, in which reactionary forces were forever hindering and delaying the final good. And what is Great Britain's contribution as the larger imperial unit but simply a composite made up of elements contributed by the nations forming the United Kingdom? England, Scotland, Wales, Ireland—all these sent forth their meeting streams of national life, deep-flowing with the most passionate patriotism; and every national trait, every national virtue, however narrow and provincial it may now seem to have been, was nevertheless a real and providential contribution to the larger unit, and finally a distinct and worthy complement in the sum of civilization.

Just what patriotism is in the realm of political life, such is denominational loyalty in the realm of the Christian religion. St. Paul speaks of the "many-colored wisdom of God"; and every denomination that has a right to be, every denomination that stands for principles which are true complements in the manifold or many-colored wisdom of God, manifests at once that self-integrity which is the token of sincerity, and that loyalty to Christ which is the testimony of faith, by the courageous support and promulgation of its corner-stone principles. And the Methodist Protestant Church is builded four-square, on a four-cornered foundation. The right of appeal, the right of representation for the people in every unit of government, the right of private judgment in matters of religion, the right of free speech in every public arena—these are the fundamentals for which our fathers fought. And to-day, as truly as in the beginning, the Methodist Protestant Church is the real and only champion of these rights in the arena of American Methodism. Our banners answer true to every challenge of freedom in the religious world, even as the Stars and Stripes answer true to every challenge of freedom in the political world. And while our every pulpit oracle should proclaim first of all the Christ and him crucified, lifting up the Cross as the central figure of human history, and making Calvary the holy mountain of our faith, yet, as a companion message for this new day, every pulpit oracle should proclaim, with constant fidelity and with triumphal enthusiasm, the embattled principles of religious liberty bequeathed as a sacred legacy. It is high time for the Methodist Protestant Church to proclaim her principles, instead of apologizing for them.

The Christian Church has been required to answer the challenge of the world in every passing age, and, in certain great epochs, the whole burden of humanity has been laid at the door of the Church. In the early morning of Christian history, the newborn Saul of Tarsus heard across the boundary line between Europe and Asia the cry of a newborn hunger after God: "Come over into Macedonia and help us!" And, recognizing that voice as the challenge of the Gentile world, the great apostle answered true with a gospel message broad and deep as the primal needs of humanity. In a later period came the challenge of Nero and his pagan Rome; but the Church, in that awful crisis, followed the Master's divine example, and humbled herself, and became obedient unto persecution and death; wherefore God exalted the Church even as he had exalted her crucified Saviour, and laid the sword of Rome and the glory of Rome on the altar of Christian faith. In the Dark Ages, when pagan savagery and superstition had blinded the eyes of reason and faith, the Church was aroused from her long slumber by the trumpet-call of a new evangel, and arose in the might of God, to champion the cause of freedom and humanity and to make windows of hope in all the dungeons of Europe.

But in our own times the Christian Church is confronted with a new challenge. The nations of the earth are standing to-day with uncovered heads, in the midst of a strange uncertain calm, after the fiercest whirlwind of war the world has ever known. And in this epoch-making hour, the torn and bleeding nations of Europe, together with the emancipated peoples who are striving to enter upon the highways of freedom and independence, are turning to the Christian Church for a satisfying answer to the living questions of a new world. The Church of the days of Paul met and answered this question: "Have you a religion that can break the power of sin and of death?" The Christian Church of the days of John Huss met and answered this question: "Have you a Gospel that can break the bondage of error and corruption, and open the dawn of heaven in the midnight of superstition?" The Christian Church of our own day is called upon to answer this question: "Are you able to banish tyranny from the whole wide world, and have you the courage to identify tyranny in the high places of the Church itself, and to condemn and overthrow every semblance of tyranny, in Church and State alike?"

But our denominational boards and institutions, our historic achievements, and even the fundamental principles of our democratic Methodism, depend for their ultimate success upon our full surrender to the spiritual claims of the kingdom of Christ. Our true and holy mission must forever voice itself in the great evangel, and every watchman on the walls of our beloved Zion must forever cry, "Behold the Lamb of God that taketh away the sin of the world!" In his book entitled "The Making of an American," Jacob Riis tells the world how he knew that he had finally become an American. He was sojourning for a time in his native Denmark, and a serious illness in the old home threatened his very life. But he passed the crisis, and was sitting at an open window, looking out upon the sea, the after-weakness of the fever still upon him. And then, swift in its influence as a beam in darkness, the American flag was unfurled on a passing ship; and the sick man was seized with a mania of joy and gladness, insomuch that the members of the household concluded that his reason was dethroned. But Jacob Riis knew in this high moment that the making of an American was really completed, because his heart thrilled with patriotic joy and pride at the first glimpse of "Old Glory."

The Christian churches of to-day, aided by the undying moral forces of every age, are engaged in the heroic task of making a new world; and every true native land in all the earth is striving to make, out of the warp and woof of the races, a new nation dedicated to the common interests of humanity and to the righteousness of God. The cross of Calvary is the symbol of this glorious task; the rallying standard of all the hosts of the kingdom of heaven; and the emblem and earnest of the final victory of the Christ, as the head over all things to the Church and as the Divine Ruler of all the powers that be. And the supreme test of the Christian leader in every province of the kingdom of God, the supreme test of creeds and conferences, the supreme test of the world-wide communion and of every individual Christian, is found in the answering thrill of the heart when the cross of Christ appears; the cross on Calvary, seen in the vision of faith as the symbol of salvation; and the cross of duty, as it comes to us in the self-denying task of the passing day. May the Holy Spirit quicken our hearts to the cry of a lost and groping world, and to the answering light of hope that shines from Calvary! May our own beloved Zion, giving God the glory for the achievements of yesterday, and devoting herself, with all the joy of willing service, to the living opportunities of to-day, now dedicate her every talent and her every crown-jewel to the task of making the world's to-morrow a day of welcome to the Son of man.

XXI

STORY OF THE CONFERENCES

THE NORTH CAROLINA CONFERENCE

IN the evolution of annual conferences, North Carolina holds the honor of seniority, that conference having been organized December 19, 1828, the charter members comprising eight ministers, with whom were associated at this opening session, twelve lay-delegates and five licensed preachers. Only three circuits were formed at this time; but so rapid and constant has been the development of Democratic Methodism in the Old North State that it now stands second in membership among the conferences having a present enrollment of more than twenty-four thousand members, with two hundred thirty-two churches, and sixty-two ministers. The enthusiastic interest of the North Carolina fathers of Democratic Methodism hastened the organization of other annual conferences. The controversy between the conservatives and the progressives of North Carolina turned upon certain grievances which were so keenly felt as to have been made the subject of appeal to several General Conferences of the mother church. The itinerants themselves felt the autocratic hand of bishops and presiding elders; local ministers, in turn, resented their exclusion from all the rights and privileges of the governing bodies of the Church; and all liberal Methodists alike recognized, in common with their fellow reformers throughout the country, the absolute injustice of excluding the lay-membership of the Church from any vote or voice in the annual or general conferences. Prompted by the sentiments growing out of these conditions, a "Union Society" was organized at Roanoke, November 6, 1824, William Price, a revolutionary patriot being the presiding officer, and the membership of the Society including not only laymen of large influence, but eleven ordained ministers. Prominent among the members of this Union Society, was Rev. W. W. Hill, whose pen contributed many brilliant articles through the columns of "Mutual Rights," and who, because of his forceful activities in the good cause, was among the first to be brought to trial for "inveighing against the government of the Church." This faithful confessor, Rev. W. W. Hill, became the first President of the North Carolina Conference.

Under the ecclesiastical whip of the anti-reform minister of Roanoke Circuit, seven ministers were given notice that they must stop patronizing "Mutual Rights," and dissolve their Union Society, or else prepare for trial before the committee, the minister giving as his authority for this course the fact that the General Conference of the Methodist Episcopal Church, meeting in Pittsburgh in 1828, had refused to listen to the appeal for restoration of Dennis B. Dorsey and William C. Poole, who had been expelled by the Baltimore Conference. These seven ministers of course refused to comply with this arbitrary injunction; and these seven apostles of reform in North Carolina fulfilled a career of courage which reminds one of the seven bishops of England, who went willingly to the Tower of London, rather than surrender the cause of freedom to the hierarchy of their own day. These men were cited to appear at Shady Grove Meeting House October 4, 1828; and though not the faintest shadow rested upon either their personal character or their administrative ability, they were severally called up, charged, found guilty, and excommunicated from the Gospel Ministry. The venerable William Price, just before the sentence of excommunication was to be passed upon him, addressed the President and the Conference in these words: "I am seventy-four years old, have been a Methodist about fifty years. I was three years a soldier in the Revolutionary War; and, while a prisoner, a British officer offered me a great bribe to join the British, and fight against my country. I told him if I had one hundred lives, I would lose them all in fighting for my liberty and my country. I have considered well my situation, and am firm in my purpose. I shall not forsake the Union Society."

The blended heroism and humility of these North Carolina brethren is happily voiced in the following excerpt from the memorial which they sent to the Methodist Episcopal General Conference of 1824:

"Brethren, we modestly and affectionately tell you that we ask not as a privilege, but claim as a right which we never expect to relinquish, namely, a voice in making the laws by which we are to be governed."

One of the pioneers of the Methodist Protestant Church in North Carolina was William Henry Wills, who gave fifty-eight years of splendid service in the ministry of the North Carolina Conference. The only child of a prosperous merchant of Tarboro, he was left by the early death of his father to the care and support of his widowed mother, but owed much of his training to the wise counsel of Spencer D. Collins, a kinsman.

William Henry Wills was converted in 1830; licensed

to preach April 18, 1831; preached his first sermon in the old Hebron Church, Edgecomb County, May 22, 1831; was president of the North Carolina Conference five consecutive years; represented the North Carolina Conference in the General Conference seven times, thus giving him a membership in the General Conference for a period of twenty-eight years. It is said that William Henry Wills was the first Annual Conference President to introduce a thoroughly organized system of visiting and supervising the separate fields of labor throughout the district. The family of this remarkable leader of Democratic Methodism in North Carolina is still nobly represented in the Methodist Protestant Church. His oldest son, Richard Henry Wills, entered the ministry in the North Carolina Conference in his twentieth year, continuing in faithful and fruitful service to the Church until the time of his death in his fifty-sixth year. And Mr. J. Norman Wills of Greensboro, North Carolina, so well known throughout the Methodist Protestant Church as a member of the Board of Foreign Missions, as a wise and enthusiastic champion of our foreign fields, and as a safe and loyal counselor in every progressive movement of our denomination, is the son of Rev. Richard Henry Wills, and a grandson of Rev. William Henry Wills.

Presidents of the North Carolina Conference of the last two decades, beginning with the present incumbent, are R. M. Andrews, G. W. Holmes, C. A. Cecil, W. E. Swain, T. M. Johnson, C. L. Whitaker, W. F. Kennett, W. A. Bunch.

The names of the ministers and laymen who have represented the North Carolina Conference in the General Conference during the last twenty years are as follows:

Ministers—T. M. Johnson, C. L. Whitaker, W. A. Bunch, T. J. Ogburn, J. F. McCulloch, R. M. Andrews, J. D. Williams, C. A. Cecil, J. R. Hutton, Wm. Porter, W. E. Swain, J. S. Williams, A. G. Dixon, N. G. Bethea, G. W. Holmes, W. F. Kennett, G. F. Millaway, C. W. Bates, C. E. Forlines, H. Powell.

Laymen—J. Norman Wills, S. R. Harris, W. P. Pickett, Dr. R. H. Speight, Dr. I. N. McClean, A. M. Rankin, Prof. J. Allen Holt, Charles Ross, A. A. Hicks, R. T. Pickens, T. A. Hunter, W. R. Goley, A. J. Harris, J. E. Swain, W. C. Hammer, O. R. Cox, G. E. Matthews, J. D. Ross, J. H. Harrison, V. W. Idol, R. M. Cox, Stanley Whitaker, J. M. Milliken, H. A. Garrett, L. L. Wren, A. H. Evans, W. L. Ward, R. F. Williams.

The Methodist Protestant Children's Home is located at High Point, North Carolina, and, while it is a denominational institution, open to the children of any conference or congregation within the bounds of the Church, this institution was really cradled by the North Carolina Conference. It is a splendid and beautiful home, and, from the moment of the laying of the corner stone in November, 1912, up to the present time, it has had a most healthful and promising growth, both as an asylum for the homeless, and as an efficient school for the training of the minds and hearts of the children committed to its care. Further reference to this institution will be found elsewhere in this volume.

THE MARYLAND CONFERENCE

The Maryland Annual Conference was organized in Baltimore, April 2, 1829, only three months and fourteen days after the organization of the North Carolina. Rev. Nicholas Snethen became the first president of the Maryland; and this was a mutual honor to the man and the conference, for while Mr. Snethen is really the first among equals in the bright galaxy of the fathers and founders of the Methodist Protestant Church, the Maryland Conference, by her constant fruit-bearing in the Lord's vineyard, and by her industrious development of progressive institutions, has fully justified the honor of having had this great leader for her first presiding officer.

The local fields of the Maryland Conference territory have responded faithfully to the plowmen and the seed-sowers of Democratic Methodism. Only twenty ordained ministers and twenty-six lay-delegates were enrolled on that historic day in 1829, but to-day the Maryland has thirty-five thousand members; one hundred and fifty itinerant ministers and preachers, with sixty-three un-stationed ministers and preachers; and one hundred and fifty pastoral charges, which, because of the sub-divisions of circuits into separate churches, brings the number of appointments to two hundred and eighty-nine.

Baltimore has been the scene of decisive events throughout the entire history of American Methodism. In that city the Methodist Episcopal Church was organized in 1784, and in that city, after a few short years, arose the great controversy from which emerged the Methodist Protestant Church. And while there was many a noble combat in behalf of liberty and mutual rights in other quarters, Baltimore was the first broad battlefield of Democratic Methodism, and upon the Reformers in that city were poured the first vials of wrath from the hands of the hierarchy. Eleven preachers and twenty-two laymen were expelled from the Methodist Episcopal Church for no other offense than that of taking their manful share in the honorable discussion of the rights of the people in church government, and in a truly Christian protest against those who presumed to be lords over God's heritage.

We republish here the names of the thirty-three who thus suffered for their devotion to the cause of religious liberty; and these names constitute a genuine roll of honor, for both these and their fellow-confessors in Cincinnati and Pittsburgh, in Greensboro and Lynchburg, with every humble champion of mutual rights in all the territory of American Methodism, were as truly leading spirits in the world-wide cause of religious liberty as were the moral heroes of old. The names of the thirty-three heroes are these:

Samuel K. Jennings, Daniel E. Reese, James R. Williams, William Kesley, Thomas McCormick, Luther J. Cox, John S. Reese, John C. French, Reuben T. Boyd, John Valiant, Alexander McCaine; John Chappell, John J. Harrod, Wesley Starr, John Kennard, William K. Boyle, Arthur Emmerson, Ebenezer Strahan, John H. W. Hawkins, Thomas Patterson, Samuel Krebs, Thomas Parson, Thomas Jarrett, John Gephart, Jr., John P. Howard, Levi R. Reese, Lambert Thomas, Samuel Jarrett, James R. Forman, George Northerman, Samuel Thompson, Samuel Guest, John P. Paul.

And we reproduce here also, as being essential to a proper realization of the burden borne by these pioneers of Democratic Methodism, the unimpeachable evidence of the unfairness of the whole procedure against the Reformers. Rev. James R. Williams, a trustworthy historian, of the mutual-rights controversy, says:

"The preachers carried up their cases to the District Conference that sat on the 26th of December, 1827, which was their proper court of trial. Here they expected to have justice done them, as a majority of the conference were Reformers. But on the morning of the second day, after holding a caucus the preceding evening, the presiding elder, with a minority of the conference, and the votes of nine colored men, who were not entitled to a vote, dissolved the district conference, and ordered the preachers to appear at the Quarterly Conference and stand their trials. Indignant at this unexpected *act of injustice,* the preachers determined not to appear before the Quarterly Conference, but to appeal to the approaching annual conference against the arbitrary and illegal proceedings of the presiding elder. In the meantime, the Quarterly Conference expelled them all."

The "Memorial Roll" of the Maryland Conference comprises about one hundred and forty names, and many of these names loom large even in the annals of the whole Methodist Protestant Church. Among the departed leaders who reached denominational proportions, and whose achievements are written into the very life-story of the Church, are the following:

Francis Waters, William C. Lipscomb, George D. Hamilton, Daniel Evans Reese, John Smith Reese, Eli Henkle, Josiah Varden, Augustus Webster, Daniel Webster Bates, James Thomas Ward, Robert Luther Lewis, Joseph Thomas Murray, Lawrence Webster Bates, Benjamin Franklin Benson, Edward Jacob Drinkhouse, John Jackson Murray, William Simm Hammond, David Wilson, Silas Bruce Southerland.

Two of our great educational institutions, the Western Maryland College and the Westminster Theological Seminary, are situated within the bounds of the Maryland Conference, and their heroic and progressive history has been very largely due to the loyal coöperation and the constant liberality of the Maryland Conference; but these institutions are considered in the educational chapters of this work.

Presidents of the Maryland, serving within the last twenty years, beginning with the present incumbent, are these: James H. Straughn, L. F. Warner, J. S. Bowers, J. M. Sheridan, F. T. Little, A. D. Melvin and J. D. Kinzer.

The Maryland representatives in the General Conference during the past twenty years are as follows:

Ministers—T. H. Lewis, F. T. Little, F. T. Tagg, H. L. Elderdice, J. D. Kinzer, W. R. Graham, J. M. Holmes, W. M. Strayer, J. M. Gill, J. W. Kirk, J. L. Mills, S. B. Tredway, J. M. Sheridan, W. S. Phillips, F. C. Klein, G. W. Haddaway, T. R. Woodford, J. S. Bowers, F. T. Benson, J. W. Trout, J. H. Straughn, L. F. Warner, T. O. Crouse, A. N. Ward, E. D. Stone, R. L. Shipley, G. I. Humphreys, E. C. Makoskey, Louis Randall, W. A. Melvin, W. H. Litsinger, E. H. Van Dyke.

Laymen—J. P. Fisher, J. W. Hering, T. A. Murray, Daniel Baker, Dr. J. T. Atkinson, J. H. Ronerts, E. S. Adkins, C. A. Benjamin, Dr. E. B. Fenby, J. D. Cathell, J. N. Warfield, J. G. Rockwood, W. O. Atwood, J. F. Harper, L. W. Hurley, T. E. Harrison, W. E. Sheppard, A. B. Stine, C. W. Simpson, H. T. Mason, W. B. Usilton, H. K. Muller, G. W. Dexter, Dr. J. B. Jones, J. Bibb Mills, A. R. Lewis, F. M. Wilson, T. D. Bowers, F. P. Adkins, J. T. Norris, W. W. Smith, J. H. Elliott, J. P. Dodge, M. A. Davis, E. E. Wooden, E. G. Cover, J. A. Baker.

THE OHIO CONFERENCE

Thursday, August 29, 1918, has become an historic landmark in the Methodist Protestant Church; for on that date, by the happy consummation of the act of union passed by the two separate bodies, the Ohio Annual Conference and the Muskingum Annual Conference became forever one.

The Ohio was the older conference, having been organized October 15, 1829; and therefore both the name of the state and the seniority of the one conference led to an immediate and unquestioned decision to call the united body the Ohio Conference, the Muskingum brethren themselves not only cheerfully acquiescing in this name but even suggesting it. The great event took place in the auditorium of the Ohio Conference Camp Grounds. The two conferences met as distinct bodies on Wednesday, August 28, for the transaction of business necessary to the closing of the career of separation; and when the appointed time had arrived, the members of the Muskingum Conference marched to the auditorium, where the Ohio Conference awaited them, and where, the president of the General Conference presiding, a brief service appropriate to the occasion was held. After the singing of the hymn, "Faith of Our Fathers," the two conferences read responsively from the Book of Psalms, the Ohio Conference reading the first verse in concert, the Muskingum the second, and so on to the end, the devout enthusiasm with which this part of the service was performed making a profound impression and constituting a blessed experience. A brief prayer followed the responsive reading, and President S. W. Rosenberger, D.D., of the Muskingum Conference, then moved that the union of the conferences already enacted by separate votes, should be finally consummated. President M. R. Stover, D.D., of the Ohio Conference, seconded the motion; and the president of the General Conference, from the platform between the two annual conference presidents, put the motion to a rising vote; and every man of the united body arose in joyful acquiescence in this progressive and happy consummation. And then, while yet standing, everybody joined in singing:

> "Blest be the tie that binds
> Our hearts in Christian love."

During the singing the two conferences, having thus far been seated in separate sections of the auditorium, united in a general handshaking, at the same time commingling, the one conference with the other, each brother being finally seated at whatever place the close of the singing found him. The separate identity of the two conferences was in this manner gloriously lost forever, and every vestige of Muskingum self-consciousness and of Ohio self-consciousness was swept away on the tidal wave of perfect harmony and love which accompanied the singing of that ancient and noble song. The Greater Ohio Conference formed by this happy union cannot take its proper place in the story of the conferences however, without a brief survey of the two component organizations, the old Ohio, and the old Muskingum. The original Ohio Conference, in the first epoch of its history, comprised most of the territory west of the Allegheny Mountains, and the gathering of ministers and laymen which effected the organization of that body in Cincinnati represented congregations as far east as Pittsburgh and as far west as Illinois. And Illinois, in that day, was well within the frontier regions of America. At this first session of the conference, Rev. Asa Shinn was elected President, and twelve elders and two deacons were ordained, and twenty-two regular traveling ministers and preachers were stationed throughout the district. So great was the faith of this new born conference, that, while a few of the preachers were appointed to circuits and stations already established, a number were appointed to uncharted regions with the hard task of carving out circuits and stations for themselves, with no missionary funds to aid them.

The degree of success attained by these noble pioneers of the Ohio Conference is evidenced by the rapid growth of the membership, as well as by constant increase in the number of stations and circuits. At the second session of the conference, which was also held in Cincinnati, and of which Rev. Cornelius Springer was president, the reported membership was three thousand seven hundred and ninety-one; at the third session, held in Zanesville, Dr. George Brown being president, the membership had increased to five thousand six hundred and sixty; at the fourth session, held in Pittsburgh, Dr. Brown being re-elected president, the membership had grown to seven thousand seven hundred and fourteen, and there were eighteen accessions to the ministry of the conference, and at the fifth session of this progressive conference the membership had reached the encouraging number of ten thousand three hundred and forty-eight. In the territory then covered by the original Ohio Conference, we now have a membership of at least seventy thousand, and in the several conferences dividing among them the great region once included in the Ohio Conference, we have leaders just as devoted, just as zealous, just as talented, as were the noble fathers of long ago.

The Muskingum Conference was organized in 1843, being set off from the Pittsburgh Conference, the combined territory of these two conferences having run a history of ten years under the name of the Pittsburgh Conference. The Muskingum very soon became one of the most thriving and progressive conferences of the denomination, and lived to celebrate her Diamond Jubilee at Mount Vernon in 1917. Great events and great names in our church history are associated with the Muskingum Conference. The "Methodist Recorder," then bearing the name of the "Western Recorder," had its beginning near Zanesville, within the bounds of the old Muskingum, and the West Lafayette College, after a brief but useful career, was developed into a home for aged Methodist Protestants, whose doors are now open wide to old folks of the entire denomination.

The first President of the Muskingum Conference was Rev. Israel Thrapp, the most famous member of a distinguished family; a family which included also Rev. Joel S. Thrapp and Rev. J. A. Thrapp, two other men of renown in their own conference and throughout the denomination. Associated with Israel Thrapp in the early days of the old Muskingum was the Rev. Cornelius Springer, one of the well-known fathers of our denomination in the Middle West, and the first editor of the "Methodist Recorder." Rev. Dr. Martin Luther Jennings, editor of the "Methodist Recorder" from 1896 to 1913, was also one of the great leaders in the middle period of the Muskingum Conference. Others of the departed leaders, who so nobly wrought in the Lord's Vineyard in the Muskingum District, were Zacharia Ragan, J. H. Hamilton, S. A. Fisher, O. V. W. Chandler, John Burns, Wm. Reeves, O. S. B. Grimsley, D. G. Jackson, David Truman and many others. The more recent leaders of the conference, before its union with the Ohio, appear among the later representatives to the General Conference.

Returning to the old Ohio Conference, it should be recorded first of all that the great Nicholas Snethen died in the ministry of that conference May 30, 1845, while other great leaders of the early days, such as Dr. Geo. Brown and Dr. Ancel H. Bassett, were long connected with this oldest conference west of the Alleghenies; as indeed were many of the men whose names may appear in the roll of conferences which were but the children of the old Ohio. Others who lived and died in faithful service were: Jonathan H. Flood, H. T. Lawson, C. S. Evans, Ruben Rose, A. H. Trumbo, T. B. Graham, W. L. Wells, George B. Dotson, Peter Laclar, Joel H. Dalbey, R. K. Davis, and Lemuel Henkle.

Rev. S. W. Rosenberger, D.D., is now President of the Greater Ohio Conference, having been elected on the day of the union of the two conferences at Sabina. His immediate predecessor in the former Ohio Conference was Dr. M. R. Stover, and his recent predecessors in the Muskingum, prior to his own term of office from 1916 to 1918, were Dr. D. C. Coburn, Dr. E. D. Beck and Dr. C. E. Sheppard.

The names of the ministers and laymen who have represented the Ohio Conference in the General Conference during the last twenty years are as follows:

Ministers—M. L. Jennings, W. L. Wells, J. A. Selby, G. E. McManiman, D. C. Coburn, C. E. Sheppard, S. S. Fisher, J. E. Bailey, A. L. Reynolds, E. W. Price, C. H. Hubbell, Charles H. Beck, J. L. Black, W. E. Harrison, G. H. Miller, M. M. Campbell, A. O. Horney, R. E. Games, D. G. Jackson, S. T. Allen, Peter Le Clar, R. P.

Hudnall, E. D. Beck, S. W. Rosenberger, F. L. Brown, G. G. Shurtz, D. L. Custis.

Laymen—F. C. Chambers, M. Yingling, M. S. Fawcett, E. K. Yocum, W. B. Goucher, H. E. Moreland, Professor W. C. Faust, Cyrus E. Custis, Levi Falk, Charles Custis, J. R. Vanorsdall, A. N. Fell, J. C. Fisher, U. N. Kellar, A. M. Lyons, O. J. Cartright, W. H. Plum, L. E. Ellis, Mrs. Ida Dorney, A. Weeden, H. A. Sicker, J. F. Cappel, F. W. Stone, Newton Price, H. A. Middleton, C. H. Bogart, E. W. Gillespie, Jos. Corfman, E. A. Palmer, E. C. Chandler, H. E. Amos, Jas. H. Watkins, C. A. White, H. A. Rowand, A. B. Jones, W. W. Taylor, F. E. Stottlemire, Ely D. Miller, Mrs. S. C. Morrow, H. R. Carroll, M. D. Thrush, P. M. Ellis.

One of the famous institutions of the Ohio Conference and one which is increasingly helpful, both in the intellectual and the spiritual realm, is the Sabina Camp Ground, where the Annual Conference sessions are held every year, and where lectures, Bible studies and other important features constitute a School of Methods, which is becoming a great source of culture and education alike to the ministers and the churches of the whole district.

These grounds were acquired by the old Ohio Conference and had become the established meeting place of that body a number of years before the union of the two conferences; and so far-reaching was its influence, and so popular its methods, that the Greater Ohio Conference, comprising the former Ohio and Muskingum territories, immediately adopted Sabina as the conference and assembly grounds of the whole state.

THE PITTSBURGH CONFERENCE

Progressive movements of the kingdom of God are prompted and sustained, in every age, by the spirit of self-denial. Every true reform begins with the heart-throb of a hero; and the heroic nature never stops to count the cost of service in the cause to which he dedicates himself.

The evolution of the Methodist Protestant Church in Pittsburgh, some ninety years ago, exemplified, above all other qualities, that moral initiative which dares to rebuke oppression, even when oppression occupies the seats of power. And personal heroism opened the first door of protest against ecclesiastical tyranny, in Pittsburgh as in all other centers of American Methodism. The Pittsburgh Conference was not organized until 1833, and even then it was constituted at Cincinnati by a division of the Ohio Conference; and the first session of the Pittsburgh was not held until 1834.

The real beginnings of the work in the Pittsburgh district, however, antedated even the first suggestion of a conference organization. The Ohio Conference, of which Western Pennsylvania formed a part, was organized October 15, 1829; but even prior to this event the leaven of Democratic Methodism had so permeated the whole lump of the Church as to have indoctrinated many of the best leaders of the Methodist Episcopal Church. George Brown and Asa Shinn, afterward so efficient and so famous in the reform movement, were presiding elders in the Pittsburgh Conference of the Methodist Episcopal Church; and even Henry B. Bascom, who eloquently defended the cause of mutual rights, though remaining in the "Old-Side" Church, was conference missionary in the same district. Asa Shinn was the first president of the Ohio Conference, having journeyed on horseback all the way from Pittsburgh to Cincinnati to attend the initial session of that body; and then, in 1833, he became the first president of the Pittsburgh Conference.

In the earliest days of the work in this region the Pittsburgh charge was designated as Pittsburgh and Alleghenytown. At the next long stride in the good cause, Cornelius Springer was pastor in Pittsburgh, and Asa Shinn in Allegheny, while Ancel H. Bassett was sent to the Pittsburgh Circuit, a charge of so great a radius as to include Bakerstown in the one direction and Braddock's Field in the other, with a number of appointments between; and Mr. Bassett, then a young man, but afterward one of the great leaders of the Church, accounted it a providential favor to have had the friendship and counsel, not alone of Dr. Shinn and Dr. Springer, but also of Rev. Charles Avery, whose name afterward became a household word throughout the Pittsburgh Conference, and the whole denomination, because of generous legacies to the Superannuated Preachers' Aid Society, and to various churches and societies of the denomination; and whose larger philanthropies, covering at once the religious and the humanitarian hemispheres of American life, gave him an honored name in the annals of his country.

The First Methodist Protestant Church of Pittsburgh was dedicated on Sunday, June 2, 1833, Asa Shinn preaching in the morning, Mrs. Hannah Reeves in the afternoon and Ancel H. Bassett in the evening. The mere record of this important event opens wide the door to innumerable stories of the early heroes of our denomination.

Pittsburgh Methodist Protestants of that early day enjoyed to a remarkable degree the constant or occasional ministrations of the distinguished founders of our Church. Nicholas Snethen, Asa Shinn, George Brown, Cornelius Springer, Ancel H. Bassett, P. T. Laishley,

and, first of all in pulpit eloquence, Thomas H. Stockson
—these worthy names, still shining undimmed after the
lapse of generations, are written on every page of the
pioneer history of liberal Methodism in Western
Pennsylvania.

The Pittsburgh Conference has encountered the same
obstacles and the same overshadowing influence common
to our every denominational unit throughout the land;
but has nevertheless enjoyed a good degree of prosperity
from the very beginning, and in manifold ways our
churches in the Pittsburgh district are fulfilling, in a
large degree, their widening opportunities. The happiest
record of all, to the honest denominational pride of our
people, is found in the fact that in every historical
center, in every place where the fathers planted,
our churches compare very favorably, in growth and
influence, with those of other communions. In Allegheny
County, which comprehends the metropolitan district of
Pittsburgh, we have eighteen churches, with an aggregate
membership of four thousand, five hundred, together
with church buildings and parsonages, which, both in
architectural beauty and in material value, are fully equal
to the denominational average of the day.

And this record largely holds true in the farther
suburban centers and in the most distant fields traversed
by the feet of the fathers. Not alone in the Pittsburgh
district, but in Uniontown, in Connellsville, in Beaver
Falls, in New Brighton, in East Liverpool, in Washington,
in Waynesburg, in Dunbar, in Youngstown, and in Fairmont, our churches, led onward by faithful and talented
ministers, are making excellent progress, and, in a number of cases, even phenomenal progress, in the upbuilding
of the Kingdom. In Greene County, which was trav-

ersed, in the earliest days of our denominational history, by Cornelius Springer and other seed-sowers of Democratic Methodism, we have eighteen congregations, sixteen of them belonging to the Pittsburgh Conference and two to the West Virginia; and at no time in our denominational history has the pastoral average, either in pulpit ability or administrative genius, surpassed the men who now occupy these broader fields.

Rev. A. J. Allen is now president of the Pittsburgh Conference, and also pastor of Grace Church, Sharpsburg. He came to the Pittsburgh Conference from the Onondaga, having served two or three charges in that district with great acceptability, and was the successful pastor of the Castle Shannon Church before he was called to Sharpsburg three years ago. He is giving wise and zealous attention to the needs of the Pittsburgh district. His predecessor in this office was Rev. Dr. Frank H. Lewis, who was elected last September, but who resigned the office on receiving a call to the College church at Adrian, Michigan. Two years previous to this, Rev. Clarence M. Lippincott, D.D., a graduate of Waynesburg College and of Yale Theological Seminary, was the very efficient president of the Pittsburgh Conference. He is now pastor of the historically famous First Church, Pittsburgh. Other recent presidents of the Pittsburgh Conference, all of whom gave a splendid account of themselves in this important office, the names being given in the reverse order of their election, were Dr. F. W. Perkins, Dr. John C. Broomfield, Dr. John H. Lucas, Dr. J. Sala Leland, Dr. A. E. Fletcher, Dr. Samuel K. Spahr, Dr. C. F. Swift, Dr. George Shaffer, and Dr. George C. Sheppard. Dr. Samuel K. Spahr, now pastor of the Youngstown Church, has had the unusual distinction of serving in the presidency of three separate conferences; the old Ohio, the New York and Pittsburgh.

The names of the ministers and laymen who have represented the Pittsburgh Conference in the General Conference during the last twenty years are as follows:

Ministers—F. N. Foster, George Shaffer, C. F. Swift, J. C. Broomfield, A. E. Fletcher, J. Sala Leland, J. H. Lucas, C. L. Daugherty, F. W. Perkins, L. E. Davis, E. S. Hawkins, J. W. Hawley, F. H. Lewis, C. M. Lippincott, J. F. Dimit.

Laymen—C. F. Hilty, W. A. Stone, H. W. Reeves, H. C. Cooper, G. B. Moore, Worth Kilpatrick, F. F. Brierly, Wm. E. Sankey, Robert Rawsthorne, Jr., Thomas C. Miller, James Irwin, Geo. W. Burford, J. W. Knott, Harry Shaw, G. W. Gallagher, C. A. Braun, C. W. Waychoff.

THE EASTERN CONFERENCE

The Eastern Conference of the Methodist Protestant Church comprises three of the earlier historic units in the territory now comprised in this larger district. The New York Conference, organized in the Sullivan Street Church, New York City, in 1830, included the territory within a short radius of the metropolis, extending into Connecticut on the east and into New Jersey on the west, and reaching over into Pennsylvania; and it comprised also the whole of Long Island and the lower Hudson River Counties of the State of New York.

The New Jersey Conference was organized in 1843; and the history of this Conference, like that of New York, furnishes many a story of Christian heroism, and these two districts have given to the denomination many of her notable characters.

Through wisely conducted negotiations, these two conferences, together with the Pennsylvania, were finally merged into the one Eastern Conference, thus constituting one of the larger bodies of the Methodist Protestant Church, and bringing into fellowship and collaboration a splendid company of gifted and consecrated ministers of the gospel.

The territory of the two conferences is quite extensive, reaching northward from New York City two hundred miles to its outermost charge, and westward across New Jersey, and far enough into Pennsylvania to include Pittston, Daleville, Berwick and Shickshinny; southward to Camden, Atlantic City and beyond, and comprising not only Long Island, but the various churches of our denomination northward in Connecticut. The progress of the Eastern Conference has naturally strengthened our cause in the centers of population; and, while the country charges have not been neglected, and while many of these rural and semi-rural charges remain impregnable strongholds of our liberal Methodism, the last decade may be considered the cityward epoch of our history in that district. The leaders of the Conference realize, however, the importance of a still more aggressive policy in New York City; and a long stride has been made in this direction by the organization of the Metropolitan Ministerial Association, which was recently established and which comprises the pastors and churches within a convenient radius of New York City.

Rev. C. S. Kidd, who is the pastor of Grace Methodist Protestant Church, New York City, is the president of the Eastern Conference. His immediate predecessor in the office was Rev. F. W. Varney, D.D., who was president from October, 1915, to October, 1920.

From October, 1912, to October, 1915, Rev. C. D. Sinkinson, D.D., for the last twenty-seven years pastor of the Christ Church, Atlantic City, was president.

The names of the ministers and laymen who have represented the Eastern Conference in the General Conference during the last twenty years are as follows:

Ministers—Samuel McClain, A. B. Purdy, J. H. Clarke, E. V. R. Hughes, C. D. Sinkinson, F. W. Varney, W. D. Stultz, L. D. Stultz, Roby F. Day, C. S. Kidd, and W. E. Pettit.

Laymen—Stewart Beers, Wm. Drury, Samuel M. Hall, Martin Elias, C. A. Stewart, Jacob Smith, C. W. Washburn, George Coxton, J. H. Timberman, F. C. Bowker, E. H. Walton, E. S. V. Stultz, G. T. Goff, C. S. Langdon, J. W. Safford, E. H. Walton, F. W. Grohs, E. F. Baker, M. W. DeCamp.

THE INDIANA CONFERENCE

In 1839 the Ohio Annual Conference set off the whole state of Indiana from its own territory, for a new conference; and one year later, in October, 1840, the Indiana Conference was formally organized at John Burton's meeting-house, near Mount Tabor. Rev. Robert G. H. Hanna was the first president. The General Conference of 1864 authorized a division of the Indiana Conference, and the organization of the Wabash Conference, which was later known as the North Indiana. Rev. Joseph Shipp was the first president of this body, and served three years consecutively. After a separate career of twenty-nine years, the North Indiana was reunited with the Indiana in 1875.

The Indiana Conference, both in her development of noble leaders for the broader denominational movements of the Church and in her worthy achievements in the local field of service, has been recognized from the very first as one of our greater conferences. The early pioneer epoch of the conference witnessed the heroic labors of such men as Joseph Simpson, Samuel Morrison, William W. Paul, Thomas Shipp, Joseph Shipp, John Alter, Harvey Collins, Thomas Hicklin, David H. Stephens, George Wheatley and Charles H. Williams. The middle period developed heroic and gifted men such as H. M. Boyer, R. Hussey, J. J. Brakefield, Helenor M. Davidson (the first woman ordained deacon in the Methodist Protestant Church), W. P. David and J. S. Sellers. And in these latter days, the ministers of the Indiana Conference are sustaining unimpaired the traditions and standards of the fathers, and as great leaders, such as Dr. Hugh Stackhouse, T. E. Lancaster, Sanford H. Flood, Joseph Boxell, Dr. Frank M. Hussey and Dr. W. W. Lineberry pass from their finished labors to their sure reward, their mantles fall upon other men as true and noble as themselves.

The names of the ministers and laymen who have represented the Indiana Conference in the General Conference during the last twenty years are as follows:

Ministers—W. W. Lineberry, J. C. McCain, J. R. Lenhart, J. L. Barclay, M. F. Iliff, N. Vice, S. S. Stanton, J. O. Ledbetter, P. W. Dierberger, J. W. Albright, E. T. Howe, P. W. Boxell, J. C. Coons, H. L. Avery, C. J. Kerlin.

Laymen—Hiram Horne, E. E. Massey, Rufus Williams, S. W. Dungan, G. C. Shirley, W. N. Williams, Felix Blaising, A. T. Merriman, W. J. Trefz, A. L. Poundstone, Dr. E. W. Longnecker, F. A. Lamphier, J. M. Hartley, F. P. Risley, Lawrence Wood, H. M. Widney.

In the progressive epoch of our denomination, beginning a few years ago, the Indiana Conference has been found in the forefront of every onward movement. The leaders of the conference really anticipated the forward movement of the denomination in 1916 by initiating a tentative program in their own district.

Rev. E. T. Howe is now president of the Indiana Conference, having succeeded the late W. W. Lineberry, D.D.

President Howe's recent predecessors in that office were: Dr. W. W. Lineberry, Dr. S. S. Stanton, Dr. J. O. Ledbetter and Rev. J. L. Barclay.

THE ONONDAGA CONFERENCE

The Onondaga Conference, as now constituted, is a combination of the old Genesee with the original Onondaga. The Genesee was organized in 1830, but that conference was itself the outgrowth of a yet earlier organization known as the Rochester Conference. The Onondaga Conference as originally formed, was organized in 1839, beginning its history with eleven itinerant ministers and six hundred and eighty-seven members. In 1877, the conference had increased to a lay membership of about two thousand, with thirty-five itinerants. Joshua Beebe was the first president and the eleven ministers who answered to the first roll-call were: Israel Reynolds, N. N. Bort, Lewis Merwin, Peter Parslow, John Barber, Allen Murray, John Baum, Ira H. Hogan, Joshua Beebe, Noah Durren and Lewis Hubbard.

When the Rochester Conference of the Reformers finally adopted the Conventional Articles of the Associated Methodist Churches, and began the history of the

Genesee Conference, James Covel was elected president; and, although the old Genesee never became a very large body, it was always loyal and progressive, and its ministers were immediately responsive to the larger claims of the denomination. The Genesee came into being as a part of the great reform movement, when the question of mutual rights was uppermost in all the councils of American Methodism; and the nine or ten years between the organization of the Genesee Conference and the Onondaga Conference was a period of phenomenal growth for our denomination; and in the same year that saw the beginning of the Genesee as one of the conference units of the Methodist Protestant Church, there was organized a conference in New York City and one in Vermont.

The Onondaga Conference, whether in its dual existence as the Genesee and the Onondaga, or in its present epoch as comprising both conferences, has always been bold and independent in defense of the fundamental principles and liberties of our denomination, and they have also held fast to those symbols of Methodism which Methodism in the world at large has, to a great degree, forgotten. They still have the camp meeting; and they do not pursue it as a mere conventional relic of the past, but as a vital factor of their conference program and as an inspiration to the evangelistic campaigns of the year, throughout the district.

Onondaga has had her problems, her discouragements, and even her conference Gethsemanes; but through it all and over it all, thanks to the grace of God and the unwavering loyalty and self-sacrifice of her noble band of itinerants, she is still on the highway and pressing forward in the glorious race of the Kingdom of God.

Some forty years ago the Onondaga Conference called public attention to the fact that other conferences were recruited from the ranks of the Onondaga, eleven other conferences being named which, at that early date, had drawn upon her limited resources. But this was said with an air of grateful pride, we are sure, and not by any means in the spirit of complaint; for every conference will recognize the fact that such a distribution of her men, while it may be lamented on some accounts, is an honor to the conference which is thus willing to share her talents with the Church, as well as being a tribute to the discerning judgment of the congregations and conferences which seek the talent thus called into new fields of service. The Onondaga Conference now has ministerial children in perhaps almost every district of the denomination, but we know that these men, while serving the Master in fields afar, hold undimmed and hallowed recollections of their old home in the Empire State, and cherish, with unchanged love and admiration, their spiritual fathers and brothers in the old Onondaga.

Indeed, as it seems to us, a certain degree of interchange, and of reciprocal service between the conferences, must surely redound to the good of the cause and to the glory of the kingdom. Of course, however, the conference which nurtures and ordains a minister of the gospel has the first claim to his services; and he should listen, with stilled lips and obedient heart, for the voice of God.

Among the earlier leaders of Democratic Methodism within the territory now covered by the Onondaga Conference, every true record must include the name of Rev. A. E. Wheat and Rev. Nathan Swift; and among the leaders of the present generation of Methodist Protestants in the Onondaga are Rev. I. J. Howland, the conference president; E. D. Ridgeway, L. J. Reed, W. H. Bentley, E. D. Howland, J. R. Waggoner, H. B. Loomis, Henry N. Becker, O. P. Wildey, S. S. Lucey, J. H. Richards, F. E. Carter, G. S. Martin, D. Shorts, A. E. Weaver, E. L. Weaver and G. C. Weaver.

The names of the ministers and the laymen who have represented the Onondaga Conference in the General Conference during the last twenty years are as follows:

Ministers—S. E. Matthews, W. H. Bentley, P. O. Wildey, H. B. Loomis, E. C. Weaver, I. A. Brice, Ivan J. Howland.

Laymen—E. H. Coe, C. W. Waterman, Ira McMichael, Chas. Hawley, W. M. Pasco, George Dexter, Newton M. Coe.

Typical summer resorts are often mere places of sojourn, where the social functions of the city, transplanted for a season, go forward with the usual zest, and sometimes with redoubled activity. Other resorts are genuine retreats for the tired brain-worker, or the weary hands and feet; and in such places the temporary resident gains rest and relaxation, in preparing for still more efficient service in the various fields of human activity.

A number of annual Conferences of the Methodist Protestant Church have established places of assembly, which are used at once for camp meetings, lecture courses and Bible schools. All the world has become acquainted with the Winonas and the Chautauquas, where intellectual and spiritual feasts are broken to soul-hungry multitudes. At Lake View, on the shore of Lake Ontario, the Onondaga Conference has beautiful assembly grounds, which are capable of development into one of the finest resorts in all the land.

THE MICHIGAN CONFERENCE

The Michigan Conference was organized in July, 1842, the nucleus of this organization being the three circuits including Adrian, Franklin and Jackson. Five itinerants, hitherto connected with the Ohio Conference, were the charter members of the Michigan, these pioneer ministers being, Jeremiah T. Pratt, Elisha Hall, Laban Smith, George B. Wooster, Beniah Bayn. When the organization was completed, eighteen preachers were recognized, and a survey of the territory disclosed something less than four hundred members. Rev. James Gay was elected president; and these few pioneers of Democratic Methodism in the great peninsular state launched their new conference with all the fullness of faith in God and with a clear vision of the opportunity before them.

In 1858 the West Michigan Conference was set off from the Michigan, and began its own separate and prosperous career; a career which later included the acquisition of Midland Park, at Gull Lake, as a Conference Assembly Ground, this institution being still at this day one of the chief factors of present good and of future hope in the reunited Michigan Conference. In the same year which saw the separate organization of the West Michigan Conference, the North Iowa was set off from the Iowa Conference. A new conference was organized in Minnesota, and the "Olive Leaf," one of the early organs of our liberal Methodism, began its career at Lowell, Massachusetts, under the direction of the Boston Conference, this publication being under the editorial conduct of Rev. J. M. Mayall, who later became one of the leading spirits of the North Illinois Conference.

These courageous outgoings into the newer territories of our denominational field were of course subject to sharp reactions, because in many instances the zeal of the early champions of Democratic Methodism, together with the Macedonian call from places innumerable, led the advance guard too far out of communication with the main body of the denomination. It came to pass, therefore, that the same process recurred in every quarter of the country, some of these newer conferences being consolidated, and remaining as sources of still greater influence and power to the present time, while others were reunited with their mother conferences. Therefore, just as the Ohio and the Muskingum finally united to form the one Greater Ohio Conference, and just as the various conferences in Indiana were united with the one Greater Indiana, and as the New Jersey, New York and the Pennsylvania Conferences united to form the Eastern, so the West Michigan Conference was reunited with the Michigan Conference, making the boundaries of the conference conterminous with those of the state itself. The reunion of the West Michigan and the Michigan took place at Flint, in 1894.

The earlier annals of the Michigan Conference and of the sister conference in West Michigan, record the name of many a hero who followed the feet of the fathers in planting the cause of Democratic Methodism far out in the forests and prairies of America.

In the later epoch of the Michigan Conference there have been many progressive developments, including great improvements at Midland Park, the conference camp ground, and including the planting of our Church on sure foundations in the City of Detroit and other large communities, and including, most of all and best of all, during the last few years, a spirit of progress which is the sure forerunner of greater prosperity than the conference has ever known.

There is no place in America more adapted by nature to the higher purposes of the summer resort than Midland Park, on the shore of beautiful Gull Lake, the meeting-place of the summer assembly, the camp-meeting and the business sessions of the Michigan Conference. This valuable property was acquired by the West Michigan Conference, and was the noblest contribution of that conference to the Methodist Protestants of all Michigan at the time of the reunion of the two bodies at Flint in 1892.

Midland Park is organized not only as an ecclesiastical unit, but is also a recognized municipality; and the numerous cottages now owned and inhabited through the summer season by so many of our Michigan families, are safeguarded by the civil law as well as by the regulations of the Michigan Annual Conference. Rev. J. K. Reilly, who is the president of the Camp Meeting Association, is therefore also the mayor of the town; and this happy condition, this twofold assurance of law and order in the streets of this little city, makes the place a very attractive proposition to those who wish to have a cottage home through the summer season.

The Camp Meeting Association is officered by the leaders of the Michigan Conference, and the Methodist Protestants of Michigan cherish Midland Park as, in many respects, the very heart-center of our cause in the peninsular state. While Rev. Reilly is president of the Camp Meeting Association, Rev. J. A. Moray is the secretary, Rev. F. W. Stevenson is the treasurer, and Brother E. L. Hursley, a wide-awake and representative layman of the place, is manager of the grounds; and closely identified with this noble enterprise are Rev. J. H. Hescott, president of the Annual Conference; Rev. Carl Lundbom, Rev. Charles Bragg, Rev. G. N. Gillett, Rev. Frank Hemingway, Rev. J. W. McCue, Rev. Elias Wonderlic, Rev. Eugene F. Root and others of equal devotion to the institution.

Rev. Howard J. Hescott is the president of the Michigan Conference.

Other recent presidents of the Michigan Conference were Rev. W. C. Harger, Rev. C. W. Stevenson, D.D., Rev. W. H. Cole, Rev. Dr. F. A. Perry, Rev. J. W. Gray, D.D., and Rev. F. Traver.

The names of the ministers and laymen who have represented the Michigan Conference in the General Conference during the last twenty years are as follows:

Ministers—J. W. Gray, J. W. Will, W. C. Harger, C. L. Ellis, W. H. Cole, F. A. Perry, M. R. Saigeon, H. J. Hescott, Harry Godsell, F. W. Stephenson.

Laymen—Josiah Tompkins, F. A. Grinnell, W. N. Swift, Ely D. Miller, Simon Gould, E. L. Hursley, B. S. Jennings, E. R. Vincent, R. W. Leverington, Fred Dernberger, John Church.

THE WEST VIRGINIA CONFERENCE

The West Virginia Conference of the Methodist Protestant Church was organized in 1854, being constituted by the Pittsburgh Conference, through the detachment of a large number of charges hitherto belonging to the Pittsburgh territory. In the same manner the Pittsburgh itself was constituted twenty years earlier by action of the Ohio Conference.

Rev. Peter T. Laishley became the first president of the conference through the act of organization passed by the Pittsburgh Conference, the Pittsburgh that year having elected two presidents, one for the Pittsburgh and one for the West Virginia; but at the first regular session of the West Virginia, held in Pruntytown October 27, 1855, Rev. D. R. Helmick was elected president.

The planting of Democratic Methodism in West Virginia began, however, as early as October, 1829, when Rev. John Mitchell organized a class at Hacker's Creek, in Lewis County. This church was visited, soon after its organization, by Rev. Cornelius Springer, who reported sixty members from this appointment to the next session of the Ohio Conference. The Morgantown Methodist Protestant Church was organized by Cornelius Springer in 1830, with Rev. W. H. Marshall as assistant pastor. Indeed it may be said that Rev. Cornelius Springer was the pastor-evangelist of all that region, his great work including not only Fairmont, Morgantown and the intervening territory of West Virginia, but also Green County and adjacent regions in Pennsylvania. The Ohio Conference had really appointed him pastor at large in that early day, and his work was literally that of a home missionary; and with burning zeal and rare good judgment he carved out for the Kingdom of Christ and for liberal Methodism in all those vast regions the potential appointments, circuits and stations which afterward became famous in the annals of the Muskingum, the Pittsburgh and the West Virginia Conferences.

Others of the early churches of the West Virginia Conference were Pruntytown, Lost Creek and Harrisville. The church at Pruntytown included laymen of prominence in the public life of West Virginia, notably

Hon. J. W. Burdett and Hon. C. W. Newland. The work at Lost Creek, in Harrison County, enrolled Isaac Swisher, John Dawson, John Gaston, John McPherson and others, while the Harrisville church numbered among its members Z. M. Pierpoint and wife, whose descendants are still members of the Harrisville church. The Morrison neighborhood, in Greensboro County, was a birthplace of Democratic Methodism, and many places in that region are rich with the historic associations which go back not only to the days of the Reformers, but to the missionary journeys of Francis Asbury.

The West Virginia Conference has followed the example of the Ohio Conference in building a conference memorial church. This temple of Democratic Methodism is located in the City of Clarksburg, and is at once a beautiful example of ecclesiastical architecture and a genuine house of work as well as of worship.

The West Virginia Conference preserves a record of the conference presidents from the beginning, and this roll of honor discloses the names of many leaders who were not only famous in the annals of the West Virginia Annual Conference, but whose names are written large in the denominational life of the Methodist Protestant Church. Among these famous leaders are: P. T. Laishley, D. R. Helmick, D. B. Dorsey, George Nestor, J. J. Poynter, Benjamin Stout, D. H. Davis, G. W. Barrett, A. L. McKeever. Rev. P. T. Laishley was reëlected to the presidency for four separate terms of office, including his election to that office by the Pittsburgh Conference, while the equally famous George Nestor was elected to four distinct and separate terms of service. The list of later presidents of the conference includes D. G. Helmick, D. C. Wees, J. M. Conaway, E. G. Wilson, M.

L. Smith, J. J. Mason, I. A. Barnes, M. D. Helmick, George R. Brown, U. W. Morrison, D. S. Boggs, J. I. Vincent, J. N. Holt, W. H. Hart, J. J. Phillips and the present incumbent, J. Alfred Selby.

The atmosphere of West Virginia has always been favorable to Democratic Methodism; for the mountaineers of that state, and even the dwellers in the low lands, are as devoted to the cause of freedom and self-government as are the mountain dwellers of Switzerland, or the heroes who of old kept house for liberty in Athens and Sparta.

The West Virginia Conference has a total membership of something more than eighteen thousand, with about eighty-seven ministers and preachers.

Rev. J. Alfred Selby, D.D., is the president of the West Virginia Conference. Among Dr. Selby's recent predecessors in the presidency were Dr. George R. Brown, Dr. U. W. Morrison, Rev. W. H. Hart and Rev. J. N. Holt.

The names of the ministers and laymen who have represented the West Virginia Conference in the General Conference during the last twenty years are as follows:

Ministers—George R. Brown, C. L. Queen, D. G. Helmick, A. L. McKeever, A. J. Allman, M. D. Helmick, M. L. Smith, J. I. Vincent, U. W. Morrison, D. S. Boggs, A. F. Hess, J. J. Phillips, S. C. Jones, G. N. Snyder, J. N. Holt, J. P. Turkelson, W. H. Hart, Josiah Payne, B. M. Mitchell, L. E. Oldaker, J. H. Mossburg, J. Alfred Selby, C. A. Isner and Jesse R. Jones.

Laymen—J. C. Roane, Dr. J. W. Kidd, Dr. Jos. B. Watson, Fred H. Smith, Wm. Mearns, W. A. Strickler, Prof. U. S. Fleming, J. I. Swindler, Prof. W. W. Tapp, A. D. Williams, H. A. Hall, J. H. Ruttencutter, T. E. Hodge, J. H. Moore, J. P. Pierpont, Irca C. Post, J. E. Cunningham, Dr. L. L. McKinney, C. D. Barbe,

D. D. Casto, M. L. Abbott, John H. Long, D. J. Gordon, J. E. Currey, E. W. Swan, S. D. Oldaker, M. F. Llewellyn, C. A. Lawson, J. B. Westfall, Wilber Young, C. A. Short, M. L. Shields, Hugh Starcher, John A. High.

GEORGIA CONFERENCE

The Georgia Conference was organized in 1830, and was therefore very early in the field. The first Annual Conference met at Newton Camp Grounds July 22, 1830. Rev. Epps Tucker was elected president and Gen. Harrison Jones secretary. The Georgia Conference was represented in the Constitutional Convention of 1830, and thereafter took a prominent part in the framing of the elementary principles and in determining the policy of the Methodist Protestant Church.

About six months after the Constitutional Convention, the Georgia Conference met at Swearingen's Camp Grounds in Twiggs County, Georgia, this session being held July 29, 1831.

The Georgia Conference has never been very large in membership, but it has always contained a group of loyal men who have been steadfast in the faith of the fathers.

Rev. J. R. Anderson is president of the Georgia Conference, and his immediate predecessor in the presidency was Rev. C. B. McDaniel.

The names of the ministers and laymen who have represented the Georgia Conference in the General Conference during the last twenty years are as follows:

Ministers—J. McD. Radford, R. S. McGarity, J. R. Anderson, J. M. Reynolds, C. M. Lyons.

Laymen—J. J. Barge, W. C. Adamson, H. D. Moore, S. W. Jackson.

The organization of the Alabama Conference, like that of many other conferences of our denomination, was a process rather than a clear-cut beginning on any single date. A preliminary organization was effected May 1, 1829, but the names of those connected with this initial movement are not preserved. It is recorded, however, that Briton Capell was chosen president, and Seymour Powell, secretary.

The second conference was held in September, 1829, near Smith's Ferry, in Perry County. A camp-meeting was held in connection with this meeting of the conference, and the revival spirit therefore entered into the very life of the organization. Eight ministers received appointments at this conference; namely, J. D. Lee, B. Dulaney, B. Capell, P. S. Graves, J. M. McCormick and A. J. Blackburn. In addition to these itinerant ministers a number of unstationed ministers and preachers were also in attendance, including Ely Terry, S. Oliver, E. Myers, A. J. Campbell, John Meek, James Meek, J. Hawley, William Rice and G. A. Campbell.

The first local church of our denomination organized in Alabama was inspired by the arbitrary act of the Methodist Episcopal minister at a quarterly meeting held near Camden, Wilcox County. Three brethren of that community were refused the elements of the Lord's Supper, presumably because of their connection with the Reform Movement in the Methodist Episcopal Church; and accordingly, when the minister in charge failed either to correct this spiritual discourtesy, or to explain the reason for the same, the brethren withdrew from the old Church and allied themselves with the Methodist Protestant Church, becoming fruitful laborers in the Lord's vineyard.

Rev. T. C. Casaday is president of the Alabama Conference, and also pastor of our church in Birmingham, where he is doing an aggressive and a successful work for the Master.

The names of the ministers and laymen who have represented the Alabama Conference in the General Conference during the last twenty years are as follows:

Ministers—T. M. McGraw, G. W. Jones, J. P. Morgan, W. G. McDaniel, S. H. Lynch, W. D. Stewart, T. C. Casaday, W. C. Connor, G. D. Messer and J. S. Eddins.

Laymen—T. H. Crenshaw, A. W. Rucker, A. C. Rogers, L. S. Kilpatrick, Ira Champion, E. G. Jones, A. H. Wilson, L. N. Henderson.

NORTH ILLINOIS CONFERENCE

The first Methodist Protestant Congregation in the territory which now forms the State of Illinois was gathered and organized by Rev. James Sims; and he took part, also, in the formation of the Illinois Conference, in 1836. The Ohio Conference, however, was the mother of all conferences west of Cincinnati in that early day, and it was by a further voluntary surrender of territory from the Ohio District that the first annual conference in Illinois was formed. In its first boundaries, the Illinois Conference included all fields west of Indiana. In the natural evolution of our work, in that great pioneer region, the North Illinois Conference was organized in 1843, the first session being held at Princeton, and Rev. P. J. Strong becoming the first president. Rev. Nicholas Snethen attended this first session of the North Illinois Conference, and his presence was doubtless a great factor in determining the literary trend of all these initial movements of our denomination in the Middle West.

The work in Illinois soon developed into three annual conferences; the Illinois, the North Illinois and the South Illinois. And during the passionate times when the slavery question was being settled for America and the world, we had four conferences in that state, the South Illinois being divided by hostile lines on that great issue. A number of conferences in the Middle West have so united their forces as to make the boundaries of the annual conference conterminous with those of the state. The Indiana, the Michigan and the Ohio have reorganized for this purpose, and all the stations and circuits in each of these states belong to the one conference, which takes the name of the state itself.

We have always had splendid leaders in the North Illinois Conference, the earlier pioneers, all of noble quality in the brotherhood of the kingdom, giving way to such worthy successors as A. H. Widney, J. M. Mayall, W. H. Jordan, T. J. Gregory, J. P. Johnson, and many others. At the present day there are many pastors in the front rank of the North Illinois Conference, and under the enthusiasm of their leadership there is an onward movement throughout the district, with special tokens of prosperity at many points.

Rev. L. S. Kidd is president of the North Illinois Conference.

The North Illinois Conference has now entered the city of Chicago under hopeful conditions, and three churches are already organized in a section of the city which, by common consent of other communions, and by explicit approval of the Council of Churches, is entirely surrendered to the care of our denomination. Rev. C. O. Harvey, who is a great enthusiast in the planting of new churches in our larger cities, has general supervision of the Chicago work under the auspices of the North Illinois Conference.

The names of the ministers and laymen who have represented the North Illinois Conference in the General Conference for the last twenty years are as follows:

Ministers—Richard Pacey, I. T. Haverfield, L. S. Kidd, A. J. Christy, T. P. Collier, A. J. Green, J. G. Reed, W. H. Lewis.

Laymen—J. S. Addis, Jacob May, Mrs. W. S. Wilson, Jacob Roberts, Anna R. Wilson, A. C. Ruff, Horace Link, Harry K. Onken.

THE IOWA-MISSOURI CONFERENCE

The Iowa-Missouri Conference was formed by the timely and happy union of the Iowa and the North Missouri. The Iowa Conference was organized in 1846, and comprised churches formerly connected with the North Illinois Conference, Rev. William Patterson being the first president. Both of these conferences passed through heroic periods in the time of their separate existence, and tens of thousands have been brought into the Kingdom of Christ through the preaching of the noble pioneers of the earlier times in that important territory.

The North Missouri Conference, which finally joined with the Iowa to form the Iowa-Missouri, was itself organized in 1864. The earlier enthusiasm of the Missouri Methodist Protestants found expression in the premature organization of the Platte Conference, but the few adherents were so widely distributed as to prevent the contact essential to organization. But the coming of immigrants from other states, especially during the Civil War, made it possible to establish our cause on more lasting foundations. The advent of Gabriel Williams, who came from North Illinois as missionary superintendent of Missouri, greatly quickened the activities of our people and hastened the organization of an annual conference. Eleven ministers were recognized at the initial session of the North Missouri in September, 1864, and the lay-delegates in attendance represented a membership of five hundred and ten. Rev. John Leach, of Michigan, removed to Missouri in this heroic missionary epoch of mutual rights Methodism, and in recognition of his earnest and fruitful service he was elected president of the conference. The further history of the North Missouri, up to the hour of union with the Iowa, developed many faithful and worthy laborers in the Lord's vineyard.

The later leaders of the Iowa-Missouri Conference are indicated, to a large degree at least, by the representatives to the General Conference during the last five quadrenniums.

The names of the ministers and laymen who have represented the Iowa-Missouri Conference in the General Conference for the last twenty years are as follows:

Ministers—S. J. Geddes, E. S. Brown, T. L. Jeffers, C. J. Nutt, D. H. Howry, E. M. Houchens, A. H. Linder, C. R. Green, W. H. Betz, J. C. Leonard.

Laymen—George N. Newell, J. W. Murphy, J. W. Fonda, J. E. Peterson, C. H. Collins, A. M. Kopf, Myra Hume, A. L. Busick.

Rev. James C. Leonard is now president of the Iowa-

Missouri Conference, and other recent presidents were
Rev. S. J. Geddes, 1902 to 1907; Rev. C. J. Nutt, 1907
to 1912; Rev. A. H. Linder, 1912 to 1914; Rev. C. J.
Nutt, 1914 to 1916; Rev. W. H. Betts, 1916 to 1918;
Rev. C. J. Leonard, 1918 to the present time.

The far-famed Harmony Community Church at Harmony, Missouri, Rev. C. R. Green, pastor, is within the
bounds of the Iowa-Missouri Conference, but this work
is described in another part of the present volume.

THE KANSAS CONFERENCE

The spiritual enthusiasm which had planted our
cause in Iowa, Missouri and Nebraska, had its
natural overflow into Kansas; and the work of
these voluntary itinerants, supplemented and encouraged
by missionary aid from the denomination, constituted the
essential beginnings of the Kansas Conference. The
work assumed organic shape, to some degree, in 1867;
and in 1868 there was a meeting of the brethren of which
Rev. Daniel Young wrote as follows:

"Three preachers only, besides myself, were present
at this meeting of the Kansas Conference; Moses Jared,
the missionary, Nelson Burgess and Brother Crane, and
three delegates, all told. That year I did the best I could
for Humboldt Mission. Through sickness I missed the
next conference. At the session of 1870, we had several
accessions to the ministry. Here we cut loose from de-
pendence on the Board of Missions to live on our own
resources. Eight of us preachers entered into a bond,
pledging ourselves to venture out in old Methodist style
to make our conference live by its own exertion. From
that date we have prospered."

In the later epochs of the history of the Kansas Conference there have been many obstacles to overcome; and the noble men of that district have sometimes been discouraged, and not without cause. But the sterling manhood of the conference has been its greatest asset from the beginning. If in the first years the Methodist Protestants of Kansas had their Moses Jared and their Daniel Young, in a later period they had their Jacob Nichols, their Reuben Baker and their Samuel Young; and more recently still, marching with the years, always true to the ideals of the Church and to the cause of God, such men as Rev. B. A. Brooks, Rev. G. W. Lane, Rev. C. H. Smith, Rev. C. H. Murphy, Rev. E. M. Snyder, Rev. J. A. Witmer, Rev. S. W. Martin, Rev. C. J. Knox, Rev. J. P. Snare, Rev. Charles Mellors, Rev. D. M. Pentz, Rev. J. W. Shell, Rev. Eugenia F. St. John, and others.

The University of Kansas City stands within the bounds of the Kansas Conference, and the Conference leaders, from first to last, have been the unwavering friends of that institution. Rev. Dr. B. A. Brooks, who was president of the conference through several eventful years, is now Secretary of the Board of Trustees of the university.

There is a mutual inter-dependence between the university and its denominational environment. The university, entirely apart from financial considerations must rely upon the churches which are situated at convenient radius around the institution. This applies not alone to the Kansas Conference, but to all the conferences which are tributary in any sense to the university, including the Iowa-Missouri, the Missouri, the Fort Smith Oklahoma, and such portions of Illinois, as may voluntarily ally themselves with this educational institution.

And the denomination as a whole should adopt all this region more heartily as an essential zone of our denominational territory. The university is on the one hand the fortress of our Methodist Protestant churches in all that region; and, on the other hand, the churches themselves, with every factor of loyal influence associated with our conference organizations, are absolutely essential to the future of the university. In saying this, we express a simple axiom; an axiom which applies with equal force to the educational field and the ecclesiastical field.

It is true indeed that the property interests and the educational advantages of the Kansas City University are now equally divided between the Methodist Protestant Church and the Church of the United Brethren in Christ, and that this joint ownership and joint administration is to become perpetual. But for each of the two denominations this joint relationship simply increases the obligation, rather than diminishing it, becoming indeed a mutual obligation of the most sacred character. The two churches, having entered upon this perpetual alliance, have become mutual burden-bearers on the highway of the ages; and from this day forward, it becomes the Christian duty of every unit of influence in the university itself and every unit of influence throughout the two denominations, first of all to lay aside every sectarian prejudice at the door of the university, and at the same time to guard and cherish the heritage which each of these coöperating churches has received from the fathers.

Rev. J. W. Shell is president of the Kansas Conference, and is in thorough sympathy with our important denominational interests.

The names of the ministers and laymen who have represented the Kansas Conference in the General Conference during the last twenty years are as follows:

Ministers—R. T. Tyson, B. A. Brooks, T. J. Strickler. Laymen—A. E. Leary, Eli Fowler, A. L. Cook.

THE TEXAS CONFERENCE

The Texas Annual Conference was organized in 1848. But as formerly recorded in this book, there were earlier hand-plantings of Democratic Methodism as early as 1839, within the territory which was then known as the Republic of Texas. The Tennessee Conference, under the impulse of the reform movement, established a mission in Texas and sent Rev. R. P. Rucker, as superintendent of the new field. When the Mississippi was organized, two years later that conference was made to encircle not only the State of Mississippi, but also Louisiana and the whole Republic of Texas. Still later in the progressive evolution of conferences, the Louisiana came into being in 1846, and only Louisiana and Texas were included in the new organization. Those who were active in this aggressive movement of liberal Methodism, were H. M. A. Cassedy, R. W. Owens, and George W. Johnson, the last of whom took a prominent part in the organization of the Louisiana, afterwards serving as president and doing much fruitful labor in the building up of the Methodist Protestant Church in the great Southwest.

The Texas Conference at the time of its organization included the whole state; and Texas from first to last has been the State of magnificent distances, so that ministers on their way to conference, wherever it might be held, traveled from one hundred to five hundred miles, consuming from three days to two weeks in reaching the seat of conference.

The conference boundaries were conterminous with those of the state until 1860, when the Colorado Conference, in Western Texas, and the McCaine Conference lying between the Trinity and Brazos rivers were set off from the original Texas Conference. Rev. H. M. A. Cassedy became the first president of the McCaine Conference, while Wm. Daugherty was called to the presidency of the Colorado Conference. Both of these conferences have disappeared in later readjustments of our denominational territory.

In 1878, the Central Texas Conference was constituted, and later still the Northwest Texas; but these also have been absorbed in the Texas Conference of the present day. The early days of the Texas Conference brought to the front many heroic pioneers of the Kingdom of God. Every circuit rider of that day was a "prophet of the long road"; and every Protestant Denomination in America owes to home missionary pastors of the Great West a debt of gratitude, akin to that which America willingly pays to the Pilgrim Fathers who landed from the *Mayflower*.

Among the worthies of the frontier belonging to the Texas Conference in its early history were J. W. Ashcraft, H. C. Stillwell, Wm. Softwood, J. Pendleton, Wm. Elliott, Miles Hart and G. W. Chamness; and among the later heroes of equal courage were R. Boyd, J. H. Bounds, J. F. Lembright, M. F. Roster, E. B. D. Johnson, J. S. York, and J. W. Wilson.

The Rev. G. L. Garrison, D.D., who was for many years the judicious and progressive president of the Texas Conference, explains the many readjustments of our denominational organization in that region as follows:—"In many cases also the shifting population of the early days in Texas was to blame for the many organizations that afterwards failed. Another thing that worked defeat in those early days was that many of the early founders were men who farmed or made a living raising stock, and did not teach the people the necessity of supporting the ministry, and the further fact that these men making their own living in large part, could not put their undivided energy into their work."

Rev. G. W. Sanders is president of the Texas Conference, and his immediate predecessor was Dr. J. C. Williams, and others preceding him in this important office were J. E. Butler, F. M. Anderson, and T. L. Garrison.

The names of the ministers and laymen who have represented the Texas Conference in the General Conference during the last twenty years are as follows:

Ministers—J. B. Denton, W. L. Fagg, J. D. Christian, H. H. Price, T. L. Garrison, J. E. Butler, W. L. Hamrick, W. E. Grove, J. A. Phipps.

Laymen—Benj. F. Sage, Prof. C. O. Stubbs, C. W. Bledsoe, W. P. Fagg, W. M. Moody, S. E. Womack, T. J. York, J. L. Bounds, O. L. Sweet, J. P. Lindley.

THE ARKANSAS CONFERENCE

The Arkansas Conference was organized at Neosho, Missouri, in September, 1838. The first society of Methodist Protestants was formed at Cane Hill, December 11, 1830. A few members of the Methodist Episcopal Church, together with two local preachers and one exhorter, being called into conference, elected Jacob Sexton, chairman, and proceeded to adopt resolutions of withdrawal from the Methodist Episcopal Church and to organize under the Convention Articles adopted at Baltimore in 1828. In the meantime the constitutional convention of the newly organized church had been held in November, 1830, several weeks prior to the little meeting at Cane Hill. This humble beginning, far removed from all the centers of Democratic Methodism, is evidence at once of the slow means of communication then enjoyed, and of the contagious enthusiasm of those who had adopted the principle of mutual rights and self-government.

This feeble and isolated society of believers in Jesus Christ as Head of the Church proved a success even beyond the hopes of its founders; and during the next summer, a union camp-meeting was held by the Methodist Protestants and the Presbyterians. This meeting resulted in a gracious revival, some fifty-five persons being converted.

The Tennessee Conference, in 1831, received a communication from Jacob Sexton, who had presided at the first meeting of Reformers within the territory of the Arkansas Conference; and in this letter, he made a plea for the admission of this society to the Tennessee Conference, and that a mission be established for the building of the cause in that territory.

At the next ensuing session of the Tennessee, in 1832, it was learned that the Arkansas Mission had notably increased in membership, and accordingly Jacob Sexton was elected to Deacon's Orders and Elder's Orders by the one vote, while Joseph Walker, the president of the Tennessee Conference, was requested to visit the Arkansas Mission and ordain this ardent and faithful pioneer to the gospel ministry. Rev. Jacob Sexton and his growing mission continued in the Tennessee Annual Conference until 1837, when they were permitted to set up for themselves, and the Arkansas Conference was organized in 1838, as already recorded.

In the later progress of Democratic Methodism in Arkansas, the North Arkansas, the West Arkansas and the Red River Conferences were successively organized; but all these organizations disappeared in later developments and readjustments of the work.

Rev. J. A. Harp is president of the Arkansas Conference, and his recent predecessors in the presidency were C. E. Holifield, J. R. Tatum, M. C. Jackson, and D. L. Moore.

The names of the ministers and laymen who have represented the Arkansas Conference in the General Conference during the last twenty years are as follows:

Ministers—W. F. Wingfield, M. C. Jackson, J. R. Tatum, S. G. Rutledge, C. E. Hollifield, H. W. Doss, J. M. Stephens, J. A. Harp.

Laymen—T. T. Lowe, G. B. Sherman, John Freeman, A. M. Crumpler, J. C. Milner, Isaiah Smith, E. M. Allen, W. H. Nabors, W. D. Wingfield, J. H. Hearn, W. A. Templeton.

THE LOUISIANA CONFERENCE

The Louisiana Conference was organized in October, 1846, the district including at that time both Louisiana and Texas. Geo. W. Johnson, recently from Ohio, took a prominent part in the planting of Mutual-Rights Methodism in that region, and was afterwards made president of the conference. He labored extensively and fruitfully in the building up of the Methodist Protestant Church.

After two years the territory of Texas was separated

from the Louisiana district, and started out on its own separate career.

In the later evolution of our work in the Southwest the Louisiana-Arkansas Conference came into being; and yet again in 1880, the Louisiana and Arkansas were re-organized, into separate conferences, the boundaries of each conference being conterminous with those of the state.

The leaders of the Louisiana Conference are loyal to the denominational program and are organizing their charges on progressive lines of development.

Rev. E. O. Hearne is president of the Louisiana Conference, and his immediate predecessor was Rev. Enoch M. Mouser.

The names of the ministers and laymen who have represented the Louisiana Conference in the General Conference during the last twenty years are as follows:

Ministers—J. E. Gaar, Wm. D. Gaar, E. M. Mouser, M. S. Hollingshead, Mrs. Mary E. Bartlett.

Laymen—A. W. Stewart, A. T. Nelson, W. W. McDonald, Prof. J. W. Warner.

THE MISSISSIPPI CONFERENCE

The Mississippi Conference had its beginning in the initiative courage of Rev. John McCormick, a local elder of the Methodist Episcopal Church. Soon after the preliminary foundation of 1828 this pioneer of Democratic Methodism began to organize Associate Methodist churches in Mississippi, on the basis of the Articles of Association adopted by the Baltimore Convention. Rev. Mr. McCormick was recognized by the Alabama Conference in 1829, and proceeding vigorously with his pioneer work, and being greatly aided by the arbitrary methods pursued by the Methodist Episcopal Church to retard and discourage his work, he built a church at Hopewell, Jasper County; organized a Quarterly Conference in Newton County, and surrounded himself with zealous helpers in the propagation of Liberal Methodism.

The Mississippi Conference at the first embraced not only the state which gave it name, but also Louisiana and the whole Republic of Texas. The first president of the Mississippi Conference was Rev. Elisha Lott. The conference organization was effected in 1841, and in 1853 the North Mississippi was set off from the Mississippi, the Louisiana Conference having been organized from the former territory of the Mississippi in 1846, and the Texas Conference in 1848.

In the development of the Mississippi Conference occurred one of the serious episodes which have recurred all too often in the newer and smaller conferences of the Methodist Protestant Church. In this paragraph we quote verbatim from Rev. R. H. M. Watson, who has been for several years and is to-day, the president of the Mississippi Conference:

"Previous to 1870, there were numerous prominent Methodist Protestant churches in many parts of the conference district, but 'owing to the fact,' as the minutes of 1871 state, 'that the president, C. F. Gillespie, formally turned over the conference and most of its members to the Methodist Episcopal Church, South,' there were present only four ministers at the ensuing conference in 1872."

Rev. R. H. M. Watson has been for many years the president of the Mississippi Conference.

The names of the ministers and laymen who have represented the Mississippi Conference in the General Conference during the last twenty years are as follows:

Ministers—J. L. Scarborough, W. W. Ridgway, R. H. M. Watson, J. F. Williamson, C. W. Walley, W. N. Hill.
Laymen—J. J. Kelley, F. A. Grinnell, J. B. Allen, O. Hillman, W. C. Shows, A. D. Sharpe, W. R. Lee, H. T. Miller, N. S. Williamson.

THE FORT SMITH-OKLAHOMA CONFERENCE

The Fort Smith-Oklahoma Conference is the recent product of a long period of evolution in the great Southwest, and comprehends a number of earlier conferences. The oldest of the historic units forming this new district is the Fort Smith Conference, which was organized in the year 1881, being set off at that time from the territory of the North Arkansas Conference. Rev. Clark Mason was the first president of the Fort Smith district.

The first work of our denomination in Oklahoma was organized in the northeastern part of the state and was known as the Indian Mission Conference. This initial step was taken in 1887; and a little later the Oklahoma Conference, the Southern Oklahoma, the Chickasaw Mission and the Choctaw Mission were organized one by one. Among the pioneer leaders in this aggressive work were B. L. Hancock, J. E. Bounds, and B. J. Doughty. These several Oklahoma districts were merged by the General Conference in 1908, in the one Oklahoma Conference, and the General Conference of 1916 authorized and recommended the union of the Oklahoma and the Fort Smith districts, and this recommendation was followed by the merging of the two conferences, in a most harmonious way, this event taking place at Shiloh, Arkansas, in 1917.

The Fort Smith-Oklahoma Conference occupies one of the most promising fields of our denominational territory, and the leaders of the conference are wide awake to the splendid opportunity which lies before them.

Rev. M. L. Mathews, one of the progressive leaders of the Fort Smith-Oklahoma Conference, was president of the conference through four eventful and fruitful years, from the fall of 1916 to the fall of 1920. He had previously served as pastor at Choat Springs two years; at Haworth, five years; at Idabel, four years, and at Oak Grove, two years. His predecessors in the presidency were: Rev. J. E. Bounds, Rev. F. S. C. Brice, Rev. J. F. Phipps and Rev. W. P. Luton. He was succeeded in the presidency in 1920 by Rev. O. W. Milburn, who after a very successful pastorate at Quinton, has entered upon the duties of the presidency with the greatest enthusiasm, and with the coöperation and confidence of every pastor in the district.

A number of the newest churches in the Fort Smith-Oklahoma have made phenomenal progress, or present immediate opportunities which are prophetic of great progress. The Church at Hugo, which is typical of a whole group of charges in the district, has welcomed seventy-nine new members into the Church and witnessed the conversion of one hundred people, since the coming of Rev. G. O. McMillan as their pastor, eighteen months ago.

Chancellor D. S. Stephens, that famous and beloved leader of our church, is a member of the Oklahoma Conference, and represented this district both at Baltimore in 1912 and at Zanesville in 1916. Rev. W. L. Mathews was the ministerial representative of the conference at Greensboro in 1920.

The names of the ministers and laymen who have represented this conference in the General Conference during the last twenty years are as follows:

Ministers—W. S. Bartholomew, Noah I. Life, J. J. Partain, B. A. Thompson, D. S. Stephens, M. L. Mathews.

Laymen—A. M. Bramlet, G. W. Houghland, G. A. Hermon, F. S. Phelps.

THE COLORADO-TEXAS CONFERENCE

Texas is the Empire State of the great Southwest; and the vastness of the territory, together with the enthusiasm of the early leaders of the Methodist Protestant Church in that region, led to the organization of annual conferences in different sections of the state. Even within recent years we have had the Northwest Texas and the Southwest Texas conferences, besides the parent body which bears the simple name of Texas. In the still earlier period there were other conferences which gave way to the readjustments made necessary by the changing conditions.

A few years ago the General Conference officially incorporated both the Northwest Texas and the Colorado-Texas with the Texas Conference, thus making the conference conterminous with the boundaries of the state. But while the Northwest Texas immediately complied with this mandate of the highest court of the denomination, the Colorado-Texas, still protesting her loyalty to the General Conference, asked for a reversal of the former action, because of the long distances separating the Colorado-Texas charges from one another, and the still greater distances separating them from the probable meeting places of the Texas Conference. The plea of the Colorado-Texas was not in vain, and that body continues as one of the annual conference units of the denomination.

Rev. D. W. Gaddy is president of the Colorado-Texas Conference, and he made a favorable impression upon the General Conference at Greensboro by his manifest zeal in the cause of Democratic Methodism in America. He is supported by a loyal band of ministerial brethren; and, against many adverse circumstances the Colorado-Texas is laboring hard to sow the fields and gather the harvest; they will conquer.

The names of the ministers and laymen who have represented the Colorado-Texas Conference in the General Conference during the last twenty years are as follows:

Ministers—T. B. Lane, C. W. Banks, D. W. Gaddy, O. W. Milburn.
Laymen—L. H. McDoran, J. A. Low, A. Low.

THE MISSOURI CONFERENCE

The Missouri Conference, was organized, in an initial way in September, 1864, eleven ministers being recognized and five hundred and ten members constituting the membership of the conference. The Civil War had of course created confusion throughout the territory covered by this conference, and great difficulties were encountered by Methodist Protestants, as by the religious workers of every denomination. The country was desolated by the war, and many parts of the world were overrun with bush-whackers. Every type of outlaw, belonging neither to the South nor to the North on the question at issue, made the conflict subservient to their own selfish and criminal purposes.

In the midst of all this wilderness of discouragement and desolation, however, the leaders of Democratic Methodism in Missouri kept firmly on the path they had blazed; and the coming of John Leech from Michigan was a source of great good to the cause, inasmuch as he entered with equal courage and devotion into the work of organizing the various congregational units into a cohesive conference; in 1866, he was elected to the presidency.

In the meantime, Gabriel Williams made a missionary visit to South Missouri, and sought out and assembled scattered Methodist Protestant settlers in all that part, finally convening an incipient conference on October 6, 1865. There were seven ministers in attendance and a number of laymen. Several mission fields were at once surveyed and the brethren entered heartily at once into the work of evangelization, much success attending their labors.

A little later O. R. Carlton, formerly of Indiana, came to the field and proved himself an efficient co-worker with the brethren already on the ground; and he was made superintendent of the entire mission work and continued to labor successfully for several years. The first conference group described, later developed into the North Missouri Conference, and the southern organization, with certain readjustments and modifications of territory, constitutes the present Missouri Conference. Rev. L. A. Smith is president of the Missouri Conference. One of the most distinguished laymen of our denomination, Mr. J. F. Howe of Ionia, is connected with the Missouri Conference, and was a member of the Church Union Commission for a number of years, as well as filling other offices of distinction. He has been for fifty years the able and progressive superintendent of the Methodist Protestant Sunday-school at Ionia.

The names of the ministers and laymen who have represented the Missouri Conference in the General Conference during the last twenty years are as follows:

Ministers—L. A. Smith, W. H. Fisher, James McCord. Layman—J. F. Howe.

THE SOUTH ILLINOIS CONFERENCE

The territory of Illinois is now divided between the two conferences, the North Illinois and the South Illinois. But many changes have been made in the evolution of our cause in that state; and at one time, covering the period of the Civil War, we had four conferences in Illinois. The South Illinois Conference was organized September 3, 1853, and Rev. Richard Wright was elected president and P. A. Bailey, secretary. The conference includes all the territory lying South of the Wabash Railroad. The second session of the conference was held at the home of Elisha Brooks, September 7, 1852, Rev. J. L. Williams being elected president. The progress of the South Illinois Conference has not been very great, but it has never failed to recognize the denominational claims laid upon its several churches, and at this juncture there is a spirit of progress in the district which foretokens a brighter future.

Rev. J. I. Day is the president of the South Illinois Conference; and his fellow-laborers throughout the district are in perfect harmony with his official program.

The names of the ministers and laymen who have represented the South Illinois Conference in the General Conference during the last twenty years are as follows:

Ministers—John C. Coons, W. S. Coons, J. I. Day, D. B. Turney.

Laymen—John Seitzinger, E. E. Wesley, Bert Petty, A. M. Reed, Sherman Stout.

THE VIRGINIA CONFERENCE

The Virginia Annual Conference was organized at Lynchburg, Virginia, May 1, 1829, Jackson McCain being elected president. The first session of the conference was also honored by the presence of Nicholas Snethen. Eleven traveling ministers received appointments at this first session, but only eight circuits were officially recognized.

The Virginia was very early in the field among the conferences of the Methodist Protestant Church; and, with the Maryland Conference on the one side, and the North Carolina on the other, the faithful brethren of the Virginia Conference received every possible encouragement in the upbuilding of the Kingdom and the propagation of the principles of mutual rights. And the earlier decades of the history of this conference were fruitful of great results, the congregations multiplying rapidly throughout all the territory within the bounds established by the General Conference. But in an unhappy hour the Virginia Conference was persuaded to continue, on her own separate pathway, in certain church union negotiations which had been abandoned by the Methodist Protestant Church as a denomination. It came to pass therefore, that the Virginia Conference was first of all divided against itself; and, as a natural consequence, one group of ministers and churches was entirely lost to the conference, while the loyal remnant, weakened by this calamity, lost the enthusiasm essential to the work of the present, and the vision of hope which is essential to a progressive future.

A band of loyal brethren are still holding the fort, and the Virginia Conference still exists. These brethren should have the helpful sympathy of the stronger conferences of the whole denomination, and broader gates of opportunity should be opened up before them.

Rev. J. L. Jarvis is president of the Virginia Conference.

The names of the ministers and laymen who have represented the Virginia Conference in the General Conference during the last twenty years are as follows:

Ministers—J. C. Posten, N. A. Harris, J. L. Jarvis.
Laymen—David A. Duff, J. Wesley Bingdorf, W. W. Ottinger.

THE SOUTH CAROLINA CONFERENCE

The South Carolina Conference was organized in 1838, and has had from the beginning the helpful encouragement of the great North Carolina Conference, whose territory is adjacent to its own. The number of ministers and preachers is very small and the churches are few and weak. It has been for many years an open question whether it were not better for our cause within the bounds of this conference to incorporate the few churches and ministers of the South Carolina, with the North Carolina.

Rev. J. C. Summersett is the president of the South Carolina Conference.

The names of the ministers and laymen who have represented the South Carolina Conference in the General Conference during the last twenty years are as follows:

Ministers—J. M. Knowles, M. Dunn, Irwin Frye, J. C. Summersett.

Laymen—Wilson McLaughlin, T. E. Murphy, John A. Jones, C. M. Stokes.

THE FLORIDA CONFERENCE

The Florida Conference has been so depleted in numbers during the past few years as to reduce it to a mission conference; but a faithful group of leaders have stood by the work, through sunshine and shadow, these loyal representatives including especially Rev. G. H. Hendry, and C. L. Wheelus who represented the Florida Conference in the General Conference at Greensboro. Rev. E. W. Holland is now president of the Florida, and is putting much enthusiasm into the work. The opportunities are broadening in this important territory and with proper encouragement and efficient laborers for the open harvest fields, good news may be expected from that vineyard.

THE TENNESSEE CONFERENCE

The Tennessee Annual Conference was organized at Union Camp Ground, Bedford County, Tennessee, on the eighth day of October, 1829. Eight ministers and eight lay-delegates were in attendance. Rev. Thomas L. Potts was chosen president, and Dr. James L. Armstrong, secretary.

The agitation in favor of mutual rights began very

early in Tennessee, a number of societies being formed under the name of "Reforming Methodists." These groups corresponded in every essential way with the Union Societies which were the starting points of the denomination in the states further north. Finally a delegated convention of these societies was held at Unionville, August 10, 1828, when Haman Bailey was elected chairman and Richard Warner, secretary. The spirit of Democratic Methodism, in honest rebellion against autocratic government, was wafted abroad in every direction, like pollen driven by the wind; and very often the love of liberty prompted the organization of the Reformers even before they had definite knowledge of the methods of organization used by their fellow workers in other parts of the country. And so it is possible that the "Reforming Methodists" may not have even known of the Union Societies by that name, or of the "Associated Methodist Churches" by that name. And this tacit tribute to the Reformers in every community proves that they were not imitators, but that they were moved by a common and universal impulse of freedom in every zone of life, whether in Church or State.

The Methodist Protestants of Tennessee were great enthusiasts in the good cause, and so intense was their zeal for the propagation of the principle of mutual rights that they sent missionaries both into Texas and into Arkansas, until the Tennessee Conference became a mother of conferences of the denomination, having been buffeted by all the winds that blow. Our church was greatly weakened within the territory of the Tennessee because of the reflex influence of the breaking up of the Virginia Conference, through the mysterious and unfortunate maneuver which led to the absorption of a large part of that conference, under the name of church union, by the Methodist Episcopal Church, South. But the Tennessee Conference should console herself with the glory of having been the means of planting our cause in the great Southwest; and, in the consciousness of this noble achievement, the few faithful brethren who still constitute that heroic band, should lift their banner a little higher and go forward with a new resolve to preserve the heritage of their worthy fathers in the gospel of freedom and salvation.

One of the life-long leaders of the Methodist Protestant Church in Tennessee is Rev. C. I. Kelley, who has for many years been president of the conference. The good cause is safe in his hands.

The names of the ministers and laymen who have represented the Tennessee Conference in the General Conference during the last twenty years are as follows:

Ministers—S. O. Hooper, S. E. Kendall, C. I. Kelley. Laymen—B. F. Jarrell, W. E. Thompson, E. C. Thompson.

THE KENTUCKY CONFERENCE

The Kentucky Conference was organized in 1867. Individual churches were organized very soon after the rise of Democratic Methodism in America; and a number of pioneers traveled extensively in extending the principles of the Methodist Protestant Church. But the several scattered units were not organized into a conference until the second Tuesday of September, 1867, when the Annual Conference was duly organized in the home of Henry W. Rayburn. Rev. John Riggs, Sr., was elected president, and others associated with him in this act of organization were Henry W. Rayburn, Sr., Ferdinand Parson, John Riggs, Jr., Mordecai Meenach, H. W. Rayburn, Jr., and Reuben Powers. The work spread very rapidly in eastern Kentucky.

While the membership of the Kentucky Conference is small, yet the opportunity is great, and a few faithful men, including Rev. H. W. Rayburn, Rev. D. K. Leslie, Rev. C. H. Garrison, Rev. A. J. Frazier, Rev. J. A. Rayburn, and Rev. R. L. Higley are bravely holding the fort in Kentucky for the cause of Democratic Methodism.

A new factor in the progressive possibilities of the Kentucky Conference has been introduced by the planting of a Mission School at Pine Ridge, Kentucky, which is now under the zealous and brilliant management of Rev. and Mrs. W. R. Woodford.

Rev. J. H. Cleveland is president of the Kentucky Conference.

The names of the ministers and laymen who have represented the Kentucky Conference in the General Conference during the last twenty years are as follows:

Ministers—C. H. Garrison, A. J. Frazier, James A. Rayburn.
Laymen—S. D. Cox, W. N. Anderson.

THE NORTH MISSISSIPPI CONFERENCE

The North Mississippi Conference was organized in 1853, and for a time made steady progress, but the great weakness of the North Mississippi has been a lack of responsiveness to the greater denominational movements of the Methodist Protestant Church, and also, in common with other pioneer districts of the Church, there has been a sad lack of well-equipped and well-supported pastors for the promising fields of opportunity awaiting the forces of liberal Methodism. Rev. S. T. Ledbetter is the president of the North Mississippi.

The names of the ministers and laymen who have represented the North Mississippi Conference in the General Conference during the last twenty years are as follows:

Minister—A. J. Richardson.
Laymen—G. W. Michael, P. H. Wood.

MISSION CONFERENCES

There are a number of Mission Conferences of the Methodist Protestant Church among the colored people of the South and a number of the leaders of that race are wide awake and progressive in the work of the Kingdom, and very earnest in their desire to lead their people out into larger fields of usefulness. They are, moreover, loyal to the principles of our denomination. The names of these conferences with their several presidents are as follows:

Alabama Conference, Rev. E. Murray, President; Colorado-Texas Conference, Rev. W. M. Jackson, President; Georgia Conference, Rev. J. P. Tisdal, President; South Carolina Conference, Rev. H. Murphy, President.

The Methodist Protestant Church should recognize a three-fold obligation to the colored people who have espoused her principles:

1. Their denominational status should be more clearly fixed so that they themselves and the denomination at large will know that they are really under our care.
2. Every possible encouragement should be given to the ambition of the leaders of the colored people in the direc-

tion of educational advancement. The proposed college in the Southwest should awaken the sympathetic interest of our people throughout the whole denomination.

3. A definite home mission policy should be adopted with reference to the outstanding opportunities of our church within the territory of these mission conferences.

(PRINTED IN THE UNITED STATES OF AMERICA.)